SALES GENIUS

D0363227

ABOUT THE AUTHOR

Graham Jones is a psychologist who helps businesses to sell more using the Internet. He has specialized in the psychology of online selling since the mid-1990s when e-commerce began. His clients include large corporations, medium-sized firms and small businesses.

Graham speaks about the psychology of selling online at conferences and events. He is also the author of 30 books and is one of the founders of the online radio programme, *The Sales Chat Show*.

Graham is a visiting lecturer in Ebusiness at the University of Buckingham. His own academic background includes a degree in human biology, a degree in psychology and two Masters degrees, one in education and the other in science communication.

Graham is a Member of the British Psychological Society, a Member of the Society of Authors and a Fellow of the Professional Speaking Association.

`Graham Jones has come up with a great book with some fascinating insights that explode some of the myths around sales, sales management and sales strategy. It is right for its time. Most "sales training" consists of training people how to sell rather than explaining how and why the other person is likely to buy. This book is long overdue and will be an essential guide as we all lead our sales teams towards 2020' **Phil Jesson, Academy for Chief Executives**

`As a sales specialist I'm impressed by the amount of detailed research which supports the information in each chapter. Very different from most sales books which rely on the author's experience or opinions. Also, the volumes mentioned at the end of each chapter are extremely helpful and again quite different from other sales books' **Andrew Docker, Andrew Docker Associates**

`What a great read. Some sad facts about the old-school approach to telemarketing with some really great advice. Well worth the read. An insightful look at the world of sales' **Anthony Stears, The Telephone Assassin**

SALES GENIUS

**40 insights
from the
science of
selling**

GRAHAM JONES

First published in Great Britain in 2015 by Hodder & Stoughton. An Hachette UK company.

Copyright © Graham Jones 2015

The right of Graham Jones to be identified as the Author of the Work has been asserted by him in accordance with the Copyright, Designs and Patents Act 1988.

Database right Hodder & Stoughton (makers)

All rights reserved. No part of this publication may be reproduced, stored in a retrieval system or transmitted in any form or by any means, electronic, mechanical, photocopying, recording or otherwise, without the prior written permission of the publisher, or as expressly permitted by law, or under terms agreed with the appropriate reprographic rights organization. Enquiries concerning reproduction outside the scope of the above should be sent to the Rights Department, John Murray Learning, at the address below.

You must not circulate this book in any other binding or cover and you must impose this same condition on any acquirer.

British Library Cataloguing in Publication Data: a catalogue record for this title is available from the British Library.

Library of Congress Catalog Card Number: on file.

Paperback ISBN 978 1 47360 536 7

eBook ISBN 978 1 47360 537 4/978 1 47360 993 8

1

The publisher has used its best endeavours to ensure that any website addresses referred to in this book are correct and active at the time of going to press. However, the publisher and the author have no responsibility for the websites and can make no guarantee that a site will remain live or that the content will remain relevant, decent or appropriate.

The publisher has made every effort to mark as such all words which it believes to be trademarks. The publisher should also like to make it clear that the presence of a word in the book, whether marked or unmarked, in no way affects its legal status as a trademark.

Every reasonable effort has been made by the publisher to trace the copyright holders of material in this book. Any errors or omissions should be notified in writing to the publisher, who will endeavour to rectify the situation for any reprints and future editions.

Typeset by Cenveo® Publisher Services.

Printed and bound in Great Britain by CPI Group (UK) Ltd., Croydon CR0 4YY.

John Murray Learning policy is to use papers that are natural, renewable and recyclable products and made from wood grown in sustainable forests. The logging and manufacturing processes are expected to conform to the environmental regulations of the country of origin.

Hodder & Stoughton Ltd
Carmelite House
50 Victoria Embankment
London EC4Y 0DZ
www.hodder.co.uk

CONTENTS

INTRODUCTION

Sales are fundamental to every business, of course. Without selling products or services, a business dies. Sales are central to the success of every business. It is no wonder that there are so many books on sales. It is no surprise that there are millions of web pages devoted to selling. It is no shock that software to help you sell more is among the most popular item for computers. Selling information on sales is big business itself.

So, here is another contribution to that vast amount of material on sales and selling. Yet unlike much other material, this book is based on science. Many other sales books are based on the experience of some sales person or a former sales manager. They have written down what worked for them. The problem with that is it might not work for you.

Sales people buy sales book after sales book, desperately seeking those golden nuggets of advice that will help them sell even more than before. Sales people, as you know, are highly competitive and motivated to succeed. They seek out any ideas they can that may well help them sell more than they did last year.

Yet, if the huge supply of information on sales and selling had worked and enabled sales people to sell more than ever, these sales executives would not keep coming back for more. Still, the amount of advice on sales and selling keeps on growing.

Individual advice from sales people who can tell a good story and show how they improved their own sales might spur you on to increased sales. However, the individual nature of the advice means that it only works sometimes.

This book is different. Instead of being based on an individual's experience it is based on some of the most significant scientific studies on sales and selling that have ever taken place. Within the pages of this book you will find more than 40 significant, research-based studies that form the basis of the advice. Each study has appeared in a peer-reviewed journal, providing it with credibility. Furthermore, the research outlined in this book has involved real companies, real sales people and real customers. It isn't just theoretical, ivory-tower thinking, which is not related to your real world of sales. Instead, the research in this book is highly relevant since it has been conducted in a real sales context.

Each chapter is based on at least one major scientific study into sales or selling. The context for the study is provided together with a summary of what the researchers did, before the remainder of the chapter explains what that means in practical terms for your sales work.

Unlike other books on sales that are often based on an individual's theory or on accepted practice, this book is founded on fact and evidence. Within its pages you'll discover that several so-called 'facts' about sales and selling are nothing more than myth. Indeed, this book reveals that much accepted practice in sales and selling is no more than mumbo-jumbo. Companies are losing sales because they insist on using so-called accepted practice, instead of basing their operations on evidence and fact.

This book helps redress that balance, enabling you and your business to sell more as a result of solid research and science, instead of an individual's feelings and ideas, which amount to no more than 'gut instinct'.

Inside this book you'll discover that closing a sale is the wrong thing to do; it does not work. You'll also find that eye contact, so often taught to sales people as essential in getting a sale, is the wrong thing to do when selling; people dislike it and sales go down if you use it. In the online world of sales you can find plenty of advice telling you that 'email is dead'. Far from it, the evidence shows that email sales are much more productive than any other element of the online world. When it comes to sales leadership, you'll find several studies inside this book that show that the motivating, morale-boosting style of sales management so frequently seen in sale offices is precisely the wrong kind of leadership to get more sales. This book also shows you that your business needs more sales training, not less. That's partly because – as you'll discover in some more research in this book – most sales operations are not that good at selling. You might think that's because they don't have challenging enough sales targets, but then you'll discover inside these pages that sales targets are frequently the wrong thing to aim for; they can produce fewer sales than you might think.

As we progress you'll find plenty of so-called 'facts' about sales and selling dismissed as mere myth and speculation. True, sales people can increase their selling when targets are set or when sales managers motivate them. But what the research shows is that there would be even higher sales if such things were not in place.

Sales Genius starts with studies that investigate selling methods. It looks at concepts such as 'consultative selling' or 'adaptive selling'. These are two kinds of sales methods that put the customer first. Of course, sales people always claim to be customer-focused, but as you will discover in these first two chapters, customers are much more complex than we might think, so being customer-focused takes much more effort and planning than many sales teams take the time for, thereby reducing their sales potential.

The book then goes on to start dispelling some myths that the online world has helped to emphasize. Direct selling is seen as old-fashioned and out-of-date now that the World Wide Web exists. Yet research shows direct selling is thriving and has a real place in sales; so too does email, which is responsible for selling more than web pages do alone. If you are not selling via email, you are missing out on sales, big time. It simply is not true that people are not buying through email because they are swamped with messages. The research shows quite the opposite – the more emails people receive, the more they buy from them.

One thing that is clear from the online world, however, is that the vast majority of sales journeys begin online. People are choosing cars and houses online, as well as more obvious purchases such as fashion. That has led to another aspect of sales that explodes another so-called 'fact'. To cope in today's world of sales it is actually better to be small and targeting a niche than to be a big global player.

The next part of the book moves on to practical sales activities, such as getting appointments or making your way through the gatekeepers to the people you really need to meet in order to get a confirmed sale. However, research on gatekeepers shows they are much more important to sales people than you might think. Indeed, it turns out they can do your selling for you.

Other issues involved in the practicalities of sales include the need to find prospects and whether or not business networking or referrals are of any value. Many referrals, it transpires, are time-wasters. Inside this section of the book you'll discover what the research shows you should do to be sure of good referrals.

Once you have established some prospects you'll need to meet them, but many other sales books will tell you to make good eye contact with your customers. Not so, says the research. You'll also discover in this middle section of this book the other behavioural aspects of selling that are fundamental to gaining more sales. One of the key things here is the fact that the Internet appears to have changed buying behaviour, which sales people need to think about if they wish to make more sales in the 'real world'. It also means that sales people need to consider the ways in which different ages and genders buy things; research shows that different techniques work better for such people. As an example, *Sales Genius* shows that certain body positions taken by sales people work really well in particular situations. The book also shows that taking into account neuroscience and behavioural factors become all the more important these days.

While concentrating on psychological factors, this book then points out the research showing that kindness and mindfulness are significant in their capacity to gain sales. Being a hard, pushy sales person is no longer going to win customers, but the research shows that being a good listener and friend is what is needed to make more money.

How, though, do you motivate sales people to do all this? The next part of this book considers how sales people can be motivated. The research throws up some unexpected findings here; money is not the motivator it is often thought to be, neither are sales targets. Having an understanding boss who provides good training is more important than other factors it seems.

Finally, the book considers sales leadership and what it takes to run an efficient sales team. Once again, the research shows that many of the widely accepted techniques can be consigned to history. Far from needing to whip up the troops or to motivate them, what sales people need is caring and understanding and not being pushed hard. Indeed, pushing sales people to achieve appears to work against the company, producing lower sales than when you are kind and supportive.

Throughout this book you will find your ideas about sales and selling challenged. You will discover that there are new ways of thinking about sales that you may not have considered before. You will also find out that much of what you have been told about sales is, frankly, nonsense.

Using the research covered in this book, however, you will be able to find ways to sell more and run a more successful sales team. *Sales Genius* will open your eyes to ways you can find and gain potential customers, how you can be sure to meet them and offer them just what they want. You'll then be able to meet them in the real world and use behavioural techniques to attract them to your products and services. You'll also discover those online considerations that ensure that you don't let your opportunity slip past. This book will help you do all this while making sure you truly understand each customer, thereby helping you to build better relationships that lead to yet more sales.

If you run a sales team, you'll discover what you need to do in order to motivate your sales people to win more business and how you need to manage them for success. Ultimately, this book will ensure you lead a sales team using evidence, rather than merely a hunch.

Buying is definitely different these days, Shoppers of all kinds – whether business to consumer or business to business – are much more deeply informed than ever before. Never in the history of selling have customers been so well-read on anything you sell. No longer are you able to get away with giving generalities or not knowing the answer to a customer question. These days, thanks to the Internet, customers often know more than the sales person. That does not help sales take place. A well-informed sales person who clearly knows what they are talking about, is mindful of the customer's needs, and who is motivated by helping the customer solve their problem is the kind of sales person that people want to deal with these days.

If that's the kind of sales world you want to excel in, this book is precisely what you need. The research evidence contained within these pages reveals what you need to do and what you can forget. You can put those 'old wives' tales' of sales to one side and use the significant research resources you'll find detailed in *Sales Genius*. It will help you and your team sell more and sell at higher profits too.

Dip in and out of the chapters, by all means. You don't need to read the book from start to finish; but if you do you'll discover an evidence-based way to increase your sales and make more money.

1 CONSULTATIVE SELLING IS EXPECTED

Customers want sales people to consult, not sell

The Internet has provided us with some huge benefits. You can find out information on almost anything you like. You can buy all sorts of things from all around the world. You can chat with friends on the other side of the planet, free of any charges. Life without the Internet would be so much more complicated.

Indeed, when you think about the Internet from a sales perspective it has created huge possibilities. For instance, you can reach more people, sell more things and find out more about customers so you can entice them to buy even more from you. It has also made sales quicker to achieve, thanks to ecommerce. But for sales people, the Internet has brought with it one extremely significant issue. The Internet has meant that buyers are now more informed than ever before. When people want to buy something they do considerable amounts of research online. They check websites, they read reviews and they ask questions on forums. If that's not enough they download detailed information, they ask their friends on Facebook for advice and they check out what expert bloggers are saying. The result of all this activity means that buyers are often more informed about products than the sellers.

The Internet has meant that buyers now perceive sales people much more in a support role. The buyer often knows what they want to buy and why. They know the technical details, they know all the options and they understand the pricing structure. All of the traditional things that were done by a sales person are now performed by web pages. The role of the sales person has undergone its most dramatic shift in centuries as a result of the Internet.

Most sales are transactional. A potential buyer needs something and the sales person sells it to them. In subsequent contacts with customers, sales staff simply look for an opportunity to close a deal on another product or service that the client might like. But that transactional role is now largely taken away from sales people by software. Indeed, ecommerce software can even recommend alternatives, upsell and provide suggestions according to the kind of shopper on the website. The place of the sales person has been stolen by the web.

However, sales people still have an important role to play. One of the key issues is that in spite of people being more informed than ever before about the products and services they buy, this information could be inappropriate for their situation. Because purchasers lack depth of understanding, the breadth of knowledge they have nowadays could be misinforming them. Consequently, sales people are increasingly taking on the role of being 'consultants' – providing advice, support and analysis to help informed buyers make the right decision. However, consultative selling is nothing new; the Internet just makes it more of a requirement. The question is: are sales people getting the message that they need to change?

In a study conducted in the Netherlands in 1997, bank sales staff selling mortgages were found to be 'hard sellers' rather than 'consultative sellers'. This was in spite of the fact that mortgage-buying is much more a consultative process and that the banks in question had consultative sales processes in place. Of course this was before online selling had taken off in any significant way. However, a study involving 2,663 participants completed ten years later in 2007 found that in spite of businesses largely realizing they needed to be consultative in sales, most of them were not doing so. The research, conducted on behalf of the Sales Activator Company, showed that almost half of the businesses had already established a consultative sales process, but they were not following it. Fewer than one in five companies had a clearly set out consultative sales process that was being used in the business.

However, as John DeVincentis and Neil Rackham pointed out in their book, *Rethinking the Sales Force*, consultative selling is not always the answer, especially if the customer is seeking a transactional process. DeVincentis and Rackham cite the example of a company in the packaging sector that went to considerable lengths to establish a consultative sales process, only for it to be so badly rejected by the customers that the entire company was sold to one of its competitors who subsequently reversed the sales process into a transactional one. But note the date of this example – it was published back in 1999, only at the very beginnings of the impact of ecommerce on sales.

Nowadays, the Internet is the first place people go to for information on almost anything they want to buy. The transactional sales person has been replaced by the shopping cart. In spite of the advice to always match the sales process to the buyer, the consultative approach is now the increasingly dominant requirement as a result of customer behaviour changes brought about by the web.

The reason for the need to consider consultative selling is associated with the psychology of risk. Purchasing anything involves risk. We risk buying the wrong item or spending too much money. We risk buying from the wrong supplier. As a result, whenever we buy something we are seeking to reduce the risks. In traditional sales environments we do this in a variety of ways. These might include picking up the items we want to buy to get a feel of them. Or if it is a business service, we would want to meet the people intending to provide the service so we could see if we like them and get on with them. Online, much of this risk assessment is conducted by downloading data sheets, talking on forums and checking reviews. It is all part of our desire to reduce the risks.

Research revealed at the 16th International Conference on Human-Computer Interaction, held in Greece in June 2014, showed the extent to which people are seeking further information to reduce their risk of purchase. In a paper presented to the conference on the implications of 'live chat' facilities on ecommerce sites, it was shown that people use such systems to reduce their uncertainty about making a purchase. In other words, they use such features on websites to help them reduce risk.

The crucial question, however, is how do such online chat facilities help reduce risk. The answer is that they help the online sales person be more consultative. They ask questions, they provide information and they steer people towards making the right decision for them. Even for transactional websites you can see there are elements of consultative selling that work. Indeed, transactional websites that use live chat facilities tend to have a higher sales conversion ratio than those that do not offer this feature. In a 2013 study by Stratus Contact Solutions of Fortune 500 companies it was found that live chat increased sales conversion rates by 20 per cent. All of those sales chats were, of course, by their very nature consultative.

These days, people tend to know what they want and they have researched it before they even speak to a sales person. As a result, when they do speak to someone who is selling they expect the conversation to be more helpful, supportive and informative, and much less 'hard sell'. Nowadays, this is a significant way you can help people reduce their purchase risks. As the sales expert Brian Tracy said on his blog in 2012: 'Position yourself as an unpaid member of the customer's staff, as a problem solver, helping him or her to increase sales, reduce costs or boost profits. You show that your product or service is actually "free" in that he/she ultimately gets back far more in dollar terms than he or she pays in the first place. This is a vital key to becoming a top sales person.'

What does this all mean in practical terms for sales people? It suggests that you will sell more when you stop trying to sell and that you help purchasers to solve their problems. They already know roughly what they want or need and a sales person's modern role is to help them find the solution. The Internet has dramatically shifted what people expect of sales staff – but the research suggests that sales people are being slower to react. Helping people to buy, rather than selling to them, is the new maxim. That means doing research, finding out more about your customers and their needs, understanding more about their situation and the competition so that you can provide the right kind of advice, becoming a trusted advisor instead of a sales person. Thankfully, the very tool that purchasers are using to change the role of the sales person is the same thing that sales staff can use to improve their ability to sell consultatively – the Internet.

With the Internet as a primary sales tool it means that sales people can better research their customers, prospects and marketplaces. It means they can gain much more knowledge than ever before, helping them provide even better advice than they could without the Internet. The technology that has shifted the power relationship between company and customer appears to be the very technology that can change that balance back again. For sales people, the Internet is a fundamental tool to provide consultative selling to the vast numbers of web users who already think they know what they want to buy.

So what are the big takeaways here?

- **Solve problems for customers:** Consultative sales people are problem solvers for their customers.
- **Conduct web research:** Use the Internet to research your customers, their competitors and the marketplace.
- **Customers are not always right:** Customers think they know what to buy, thanks to their extensive online research – but they may be making the wrong decisions. Only consultative selling can deal with that issue.

Sources

Verhallen, Theo M. M., Greve, Harriette, and Frambach, Ruud Th. (1997), 'Consultative selling in financial services: an observational study of the mortgage mediation process', *International Journal of Bank Marketing*, Vol. 15 Issue 2 pp 54–9

www.salesactivator.com/resources/free-tools/issues-facing-sales-leaders-today-report

Lecture Notes in Computer Science Vol. 8527, 2014, pp 504–15

www.stratuscontactsolutions.com/proactive-chats-impact-chat-sales-volume/

www.briantracy.com/blog/sales-success/the-power-of-consultative-selling-master-problem-solver-sales-person/

See also

Chapter 2 – Adaptive selling is vital

Chapter 5 – Most sales journeys start online

Chapter 20 – Closing sales is not necessary

Further reading

DeVincentis, John and Rackham, Neil, *Rethinking the Sales Force* (McGraw-Hill International, New York, 1999)

ADAPTIVE SELLING IS VITAL

Listen to your customers and adapt to their needs

People are complicated. No single individual is the same as another – even identical twins have differences. Therein lies a problem for sales people. When trying to sell to someone the reaction is likely to be different every time, because the potential customer behaves differently to the previous one. If you sell to a formula, such as having set prices and payment arrangements, specified delivery systems and no flexibility in terms of options, then you just have to keep trying to sell until you find someone who accepts your intransigence. Many sales people will tell you that they remember years of knocking on doors to be told to go away until they found that one person willing to make a purchase. Ask a seasoned sales person what the 'secret' to selling is and they will tell you – 'persistence'. That reply comes from years of formula selling – having a standardized product and terms that only appeal to certain kinds of people. The sales person has to keep trudging on and on until they find another customer who fits the preconceived bill.

Adaptive selling is different. It takes place in organizations where sales people are empowered to make their own decisions and to adapt to the sales environment in which they find themselves. They can adjust almost anything to suit the specific requirements of the customer. They can take into account the particular context in which the sale is being made. They can also provide flexible solutions to customers, ensuring that what is being sold fits exactly with the needs of the client.

Many sales people believe they are performing adaptive selling, when in fact they are still operating to a formula. For years, sales people have been on training courses helping them to build rapport with a customer and to ensure they only provide them with what they want. Frequently, though, such training simply provides another formula. It might suggest, for instance, how to spot the personality types of customers allowing them to be pigeonholed. Indeed, sales manuals are full of discussions that classify customers into specific types. Sometimes these are given fancy names; other times sales people colour-code each kind of customer and some sales training links a type of wild animal to each customer persona.

The problem is that this kind of approach to sales is attempting to reduce the number of differences between customers down to a manageable group so that each category can then fit into its own formula. Far from helping sales people achieve more selling, these techniques simply provide, for instance, four different kinds of formula sales. If the person is classified as a 'Red' category or perhaps deemed to be a 'Lion' kind of customer then all the sales person has to do is to trot out the Red or Lion formula. This is not adaptive selling, it is just formula selling, made to look fancy and clever.

Research from Kansas State University showed in 2006 that customers are much more complex than simple categorization allows for. Even though buyers in the study could be grouped into different clusters, the research revealed that buyers often had more than one kind of motivation. For instance, some people in the study were task oriented – they are the kind of people who want to know what to do and to get it done as quickly as possible. These kind of people simply want to know the price, the delivery deadline and so on. The research also found that there are other clusters of buyers, for instance those that want a great deal of interaction with the sales person. But the research also showed that many people have different degrees to which their behaviour is characterized by the various clusters. So, one person may be predominantly task oriented but also want some interaction. The next person might want slightly more interaction, but also wants some task-oriented information. Prior to this research it had been thought that buyers were one kind or another – task oriented, engagement oriented, and so on. What this Kansas State research found was that it is not as simple as that. Buyers tend to be a mixture of buying styles. That clearly means that sales people cannot pigeonhole them into one category or another. Only by truly adapting to the situation can you possibly hope to sell as much as possible.

There is research that shows that by adopting an approach to sales that is adaptive, increased sales can be created. For example in a study of pharmaceutical sales people, researchers at Pennsylvania State University found that there was a statistically significant link between adaptive selling and overall sales performance. In addition, research from Louisiana State University, cited in the book *Neuro-Sell,* also found that there were increases in sales performance among sales teams when adaptive selling was used. In other words, there is evidence that shows that when companies use adaptive selling, they sell more.

The most crucial skill in adaptive selling is listening. If a sales person truly wants to adapt to each individual customer then they have to listen to what that customer is saying. This goes beyond what you might call 'ordinary' listening. It needs to include truly hearing what the customer says with an open mind. Instead of listening for key words so that there is an opportunity to pitch something, the good sales listener has to hear everything that is said and only then work out what is required. Indeed, according to the Kansas State research, sales people need to use a combination of tactics that works in each specific circumstance. The researchers said that this means identifying buyer cues and then responding appropriately.

For any sales people wanting to offer true adaptive selling it means actively listening to what is said, as well as being aware of body language, facial expressions and tone of voice. It also means being able to think creatively to provide the right solutions for each specific potential customer.

For sales managers this means adaptive selling needs different kinds of people to formula selling. It also means that sales people might need training in understanding body language and increasing empathy towards customers. Furthermore, adaptive selling only works if sales people have considerable product and service knowledge as well as a good memory. They need to be able to tap into just the right piece of information to deal with the specific issues and concerns of the sales prospect. But more than anything it means empowering members of a sales team to think on their feet and make their own decisions. Adaptive selling only works if an organization is prepared to give a sales team considerable freedom. Top-down management and centralized control does not allow for adaptive selling to work well.

So what are the big takeaways here?

- **Adapt when face to face:** Adaptive selling is the way to gain increased sales when selling face to face.
- **Focus on listening:** Focus on understanding and truly hearing what the customer says. Then adapt your responses to match their specific needs and context.
- **Raise your sales performance:** Adaptive selling produces greater sales performance than formula sales.

Sources

Kara, A. et al, *Journal of Medical Marketing: Device, Diagnostic and Pharmaceutical Marketing,* May 2013 Vol. 13 No. 2 pp 102–14

Hazeldine, S., *Neuro-Sell: How Neuroscience Can Power Your Sales Success* (Kogan Page, London, 2014)

McFarland, Richard G., Challagalla, Goutam N. and Shervani, Tasadduq A. (2006), 'Influence Tactics for Effective Adaptive Selling', *Journal of Marketing,* October 2006, Vol. 70 No. 4 pp 103–17

See also

Chapter 1 – Consultative selling is expected

Chapter 16 – Selling to men or women is not the same

Chapter 25 – Kindness kills objections

Further reading

Pink, Daniel H., *To Sell Is Human: The Surprising Truth About Persuading, Convincing, and Influencing Others* (Canongate Books, New York, 2014)

3 DIRECT SELLING STILL SUCCEEDS

Face-to-face sales still works in the Internet age

In 1949 the first-ever Tupperware® party was held and with it came an entirely new way of selling – the direct sale. The parties were the idea of Brownie Wise, who had been brought into the firm in order to market the newly developed domestic products. She started selling Tupperware® products in home-based parties where women could gather round and see the products in action in a real kitchen. It was a huge success and it gave birth to a phenomenon known as 'direct selling', which basically means selling to potential customers directly in their own homes without them having to visit a store. The direct selling movement went on to become a huge success with dozens of companies such as Avon and Herbalife joining in. The most recent sales figures for the Top 10 direct sales firms showed combined revenue of US$44.9bn and average sales growth of 7.5 per cent. Whichever way you look at it, direct sales is a huge and still growing business sector.

Some might think that because of the growth of online sales that direct selling is no longer necessary. But the biggest players in the direct selling arena have incorporated online sales within their direct sales operation. To them, the Internet is in the shopper's home, so it is still direct selling. Customers do not have to visit a shop or travel to meet someone; instead the products are there to buy, right in the web user's home. If you agree with that definition it also means that Amazon is a direct sales organization too, with annual sales that are more than double the combined revenues of the entire Top 10 traditional direct sales firms.

The sales data from all kinds of direct selling, whether just offline or offline and online, shows one clear thing – there is a lot of money to be made from direct sales. In spite of suggestions that direct selling has 'had its day' the data reveal that the phenomenon shows no sign of abating.

One of the issues of direct selling, however, is the generation of profit. Customer price expectation is relatively low; people assume the costs of a direct sales operation are lower than running a store, hence they factor that into their buying decisions. There is also the issue of peer pressure in the 'live' direct sales operation, whereby a group of people at a party can collectively decide not to spend money on the more expensive items. People do not necessarily want to be seen as overtly spending too much, so this puts the brakes on their desire to buy more expensive items. These are the kinds of factors that influence direct sales in the 'real world'. Of course, such personal issues do not arise with online direct sales. But the widespread phenomenon of getting things free online, together with the expectation that the sales operation is low cost, means there is increasing pressure on profitability in online direct sales.

Research at the Business School at Nankai University in Tianjin, China, found in 2013 that the profitability of direct sales was linked to the relationship between product quality and the returns policy. The study showed a complex relationship between these two factors that people use to determine whether or not they will buy a product, particularly in online direct sales. If a sales organization gets the relationship right between product quality and returns policy then more sales are made and fewer returns arise, leading to increased profitability. But get that relationship wrong and there is an increased rate of return, thereby reducing profitability. While the study only looked at online direct sales, there is every reason to believe that a similar situation exists in 'real world' direct selling. People would be more inclined to return products if the returns policy and the quality were poorly related.

The Nankai study found, for instance, that when product quality was high the return rate went down if the returns policy was lenient. In other words, when companies allowed people to return items without much fuss when those items were high quality the chance of return – and therefore the impact on profit – was lower. However, the study also suggested that low-price items need a strict returns policy in order to minimize the impact on profits. Presumably, people are prepared to 'write off' their spending on low-cost items if returning them and getting their money back is cumbersome. However, they are not prepared to do such a thing if the item is high priced as a result of being high quality, which is why this study showed that when paying a high price customers expect a lenient returns policy.

Direct selling, therefore, is not just a matter of pitching your products directly in the home of the customer, whether that is face to face or online. Instead, it appears from the Chinese study that it is a complex combination of price, quality and returns policy that helps determine the profitability of any sales made.

Return rates for online direct selling are a significant problem. Nick Robertson, the Chief Executive of the online clothing retailer ASOS, told Reuters in 2013 that a drop of just 1 per cent in the returns rate would add £10m to the company's profits. The returns rate within the online clothing sector is one of the highest. The industry average is 30 per cent – almost a third of products sold online being returned to the company. Some companies, however, experience much higher rates of return, with the founder of the virtual sizing company Fits.me being told privately by some firms that they have a returns rate of 70 per cent.

Clearly, returns at this level are unsustainable for anyone selling directly. Direct sales are hugely popular, but unless they are also profitable they will have a limited lifetime. The Nankai research would suggest that a possible reason that the return rates are high is because the perceived quality is low and that the associated pricing is low. Clothing retailers online have attempted to make returns very easy for people who shop online, but combine that with the perception of value and quality and people return more than they would if the quality were perceived to be higher.

This is an important lesson for anyone in direct sales. It suggests that if you wish to increase profitability from direct selling it is essential to get the combination of returns policy and pricing right. If you have high-priced items of high quality, the returns policy needs to be open and flexible. Having a lenient policy like this appears to discourage returns when people value the item bought. However, if what you sell is low price and at the commodity end of the marketplace with relatively low quality, then a cumbersome returns policy helps reduce the rate of things being sent back.

The Chinese research demonstrated the complexity of buyer behaviour when it comes to deciding what to do when being offered a direct sale. It implies that even though direct selling still succeeds, it is a delicate balancing act between several variables if profits are to be maximized. One of those key variables is a returns policy that is focused on the thoughts and desires of the customer. If customers consider the item to be low value, they will not be put off by a complex and restrictive returns policy. Instead, they will simply write off the spending. But they will not do the same thing when they value the item highly. Hence open and lenient returns policies are needed for high-priced items.

In practical terms, this suggests that direct selling agents or websites need a variety of returns policies according to the price of the item and its perceived value. This might mean, online for instance, that the shopping cart needs to highlight the returns policy, which is dynamically created according to the different items people are buying. In 'real world' direct selling such as at 'parties', it might be the job of the direct sales agent to encourage people to spend more so that they gain a more lenient returns policy. The result of that would be to reduce the rate of return, thereby improving profits. If people do not spend enough to get to the lenient policy, they are given a more restrictive returns system, which also means they will return less, again aiding profits.

So what are the big takeaways here?

- **Direct sales work for consumers:** Direct selling is a worthwhile strategy that clearly works in the consumer sector.
- **Focus on customer needs:** Ensure your returns policies are clear and focused on the customer.
- **Remember the web for direct sales:** Direct selling is now taken to include selling via the Internet.

Sources

Li, Y., Xu, L., and Li, D. (2013), 'Examining relationships between the return policy, product quality, and pricing strategy in online direct selling', *International Journal of Production Economics*, Vol. 144 Issue 2 pp 451–60

en.wikipedia.org/wiki/Direct_selling

www.reuters.com/article/2013/09/27/net-us-retail-online-returns-idUSBRE98Q0GS20130927

www.thedrum.com/news/2013/01/04/research-shows-almost-half-all-clothing-purchases-made-online-are-returned-january

See also

Chapter 6   Niches make profits

Chapter 13 – Referral sales are worth having

Chapter 29 – Customers have no idea about prices

Further reading

Christensen, Mary, *Be a Direct Selling Superstar: Achieve Financial Freedom for Yourself and Others as a Direct Sales Leader* (AMACOM, New York, 2013)

The more emails we get, the more we buy from them

The average email inbox gets 300 messages each day; sorting it all out is taking around two hours of our time, every day of the working week. A good slice of all those emails are marketing messages, trying to get us to spend more money on some website or another. Yet in spite of the fact that most people complain of email overload, research consistently shows that sales from email outweigh sales from other web methods, such as a website or social media. Even though we are all bombarded with seemingly endless emails, we buy a lot as a result of them.

Research conducted by the customer value specialists Custora found in 2013 that email dwarfed social media in terms of the number of customers acquired. Email was only slightly less valuable than online 'organic' search – the normal search results, not sponsored ones. The study was impressive because it had looked at 72 million customers of 86 different American retailers from 14 various sectors. It was a substantial piece of work that assessed a four-year data period. Over those four years, Custora found that the value of email had increased four-fold. This seems counterintuitive; as people get more and more email, you would think they would become less affected by all the noise and chatter it creates. But that is not the case. As more and more sales emails are sent out, the recipients are increasingly encouraged to spend. Far from excessive email working against sales, it seems to help it.

The Custora study is not the only research that has spotted the paradoxical nature of email. Far from putting people off buying, it seems that increasing numbers of messages in an inbox makes sales more likely. An ongoing study from Econsultancy found in 2014 that sales and marketing professionals rated the success of email campaigns as marginally superior to search marketing. The experience of the 1,000 people in the study showed that they believed they gained greater benefits from email marketing than from any other form of online selling.

A clue as to why this is happening comes from a study completed back in 2012 by the email marketing company, Exact Target. They found that people were beginning to 'segment' their communications, showing preferences for the kind of communication they wanted to receive from specific channels. The research found, for example, that 66 per cent of teenagers wanted to use email for messages from their preferred marketing sources. In other words, they are seeing email as the place where businesses communicate with them.

This makes a lot of sense. In the days before the Internet there were only three ways you could get a sale – face to face, on the telephone or via print. People didn't have the ability to segregate communications into channels for specific purposes. But nowadays you can speak to people face to face, call them on the phone, write to them, text them, send them an in-app message, tweet them, post something on their Facebook timeline, Skype them and adopt a host of other ways of getting in touch. Rather than have everything on every channel, people are increasingly separating their communications to different systems. For instance, they use Facebook to communicate with friends, text messaging to keep in touch with family, Twitter to chat to work colleagues and so on. Email as a channel is being seen much more as a business tool, the place where we get communications from brands.

In turn, of course, that means people are more likely to respond because when they turn to email their brain is already in 'business' or 'buying' mode. It means they are more receptive to sales messages because they are in their personal sales arena. When they are on Facebook, for instance, they are thinking of chatting with friends, not buying anything. The explosion of communications methods means people are segmenting channels into specific purposes – and that is good news for sales. So, in spite of the huge rise in email messaging and the massive inboxes people face, the focused way email is increasingly used means it is more likely to lead to sales than ever before, when email was more of a muddled place. People have largely sidelined email for personal stuff, meaning that what is in their inbox is much more 'official' these days.

There is one exception to this, however. A study conducted by the market research company Chadwick Martin Bailey found that when it comes to sharing information people are most likely to do it using email. They share two main things using email: interesting things or items that make them laugh. Email marketing that is either seen as interesting or humorous is therefore getting shared more widely on email, thereby increasing sales from additional customers.

You only have to conduct a cursory search for statistics about email marketing and you will find study after study confirming that email marketing is one of the most successful methods of generating sales in the Internet age. So what does this mean for most businesses and people interested in generating further sales?

For a start, it suggests that worrying about being Number One on Google ought to take a lower priority to having an effective email marketing strategy. Sure, 'search' is important, but email sales are also very important and so email marketing should not be relegated to a sideshow. Believing that email is 'dead' because there is so much of it that all customers perceive is noise and pressure to buy is a mistake. Email marketing has never been healthier. The problem with selling through email is getting people to open your messages in the first place and then encouraging them to take action and click a 'buy now' button. Companies that manage both of these things are finding that their emails outperform their web pages.

A typical web page has a conversion rate of 2 per cent – that means 2 in every 100 people click through to find out more about a product. Then, once they have the information, an average of 2 per cent click on the 'buy now' button. However, for email marketing the conversion rates are much higher. Conversion rates on emails can be as high as 20 per cent – sometimes even higher in some specific sectors.

However, these dramatically higher conversion rates for emails are only occurring for businesses that put a great deal of effort into two key aspects of emails:

1. The subject line
2. The deep personalization of the message.

The subject line is essential to entice people to open the message. As people scan down their long list of emails they are only going to open messages trying to sell them something if the five or six words of the subject line truly grab their attention. Tabloid newspapers are brilliant when it comes to grabbing attention with just a few choice words. And people trying to sell from email could take a tip from these newspapers. The amount of time, resources and effort put into writing the four or five words on the front page of a tabloid newspaper dramatically outweighs the time spent on writing the article beneath it. Yet many people trying to sell via email spend more time on the email and only a little time on the subject line. To truly grab people's attention it needs to be the other way around. If you were to spend, say, half an hour on writing the email you really ought to spend more than half an hour on the subject line. The subject line is the most important aspect of selling via email as without the right one, people will not even open your emails.

Once they have opened the message, the content inside needs to be completely personalized. It is no good simply having an email which is sent to 'Dear First Name' and then everything else beyond that point is the same. People react to emails that relate to them as individuals and hence what you are trying to sell through email needs to appeal to individuals. What that means in reality is that you need to collect as much information as possible from each customer so that you can tailor each email to them personally. It is this approach that appears to create the greatest conversion rates once an email has been opened.

The research is clear – email marketing succeeds in gaining sales. But those sales are only produced when a great deal of effort is put into creating the right kind of email that relates to customers on an individual basis. Do that and you too could enjoy the high levels of conversions and sales that other companies are gaining through their emails.

So what are the big takeaways here?

- **Email is increasingly successful:** The more we complain about email overload, the more we use it to buy things from.
- **Email creates closer customer relationships:** Start work on an email marketing strategy that will increase sales through closer customer relationships.
- **Social media will make email more important:** Selling through email marketing is going to become increasingly important as people get surrounded by more and more social media messages and confusing search results.

Sources

blog.custora.com/2013/06/e-commerce-customer-acquisition-snapshot

https://econsultancy.com/reports/email-census

www.exacttarget.com/company/newsroom/2012/04/research-finds-email-driving-more-consumers-purchase-facebook-text

blog.cmbinfo.com/press-center-content/bid/47189/Email-and-Facebook-Dominate-Social-Sharing-of-Online-Content

See also

Chapter 5 – Most sales journeys start online

Chapter 15 – Buyers behave differently now

Chapter 29 – Customers have no idea about prices

Further reading

Brodie, Ian, *Email Persuasion: Captivate and Engage Your Audience, Build Authority and Generate More Sales With Email Marketing* (Rainmaker Publishing, Wilmslow, 2013)

5 MOST SALES JOURNEYS START ONLINE

The Internet should be central to every sales strategy

There can be no doubt that the Internet has affected how we buy many products and services. Indeed, online retail sales have continued to grow throughout the economic troubles of the post-recessionary world. Yet, during the five years after 2008, traditional sales fell in many sectors. Without online sales, many companies would be out of business if they had to rely solely on traditional sales outlets.

However, online sales are only a small fraction of all consumer activity. In spite of huge rises in online purchasing since ecommerce began, more than 95 per cent of all trade is still conducted in the 'real world'. Of course, that varies from sector to sector, but even with the Internet, most buying is 'traditional'. Except, as is so often the case with statistics, all is not what it seems.

Research conducted at the beginning of 2014 by the brand engagement company Parago found that even if people do buy items offline in traditional ways, their shopping journey usually starts online. There was some variation between the kinds of products and services that people wanted to buy, but most items that buyers wanted to obtain involved the Internet in some way.

For example, when people wanted to buy toys or office supplies or cars, they went to Google as their first port of call. If they wanted to buy clothes they went direct to a fashion website. It was only in the areas of groceries, pet supplies and home improvements that the 'real world' was the first choice. Even so, for these three categories the web was the second choice of consumers.

What these figures confirm is the long-held theory that the Internet is involved in almost all shopping that takes place – even if the actual buying of items takes place offline in the real world. The Parago study was limited to consumer shopping; however, studies in the business-to-business (B2B) sector have found similar results, with one piece of research showing that 81 per cent of all B2B purchases started online.

For a business trying to sell something, it means that the sales process clearly starts online. Indeed, in a recent conversation with a client in the motor trade, I was told that until two years ago car buyers used to visit an average of eight different showrooms in order to select their desired car. Now, they visit just one car dealer – the one that has the car they want to buy – having visited eight or more different websites to do their research. Instead of trudging up and down the street, people are researching their purchases online. As you will see in Chapter 15, research by Google shows that this is typical behaviour affecting the sales process in a variety of ways.

So what can you do about it? If you are running your own business or you are in charge of your company's website and ecommerce system the solution is easy – you can change your online offering to help you increase sales both online and offline. But what if you are unable to influence what your company's website does or does not do? If you are a sales person with no control over the website you are stuck without influence on the way the web impacts upon your sales.

That is the theory of many sales people I meet. They complain they have no way of changing the website offering and therefore they are almost held to ransom by the web team, meaning they cannot use the web to influence sales.

It is a weak theory, though. There is a great deal any sales person can do to enhance the use of the World Wide Web in the sales process, even without being able to change the company website. Indeed, the techniques that can be used in such situations are also valuable to business owners who could change their website if they wanted, but don't have either the time or the budget to do so.

The first thing to do is to do what your customers do: research the products or services that you sell. Find them online. Find competing products. Look them up on price comparison sites. See what the social networks are saying about your company and what it sells. In other words, behave like a customer online and just collect the same kind of research that they do. This will give you plenty of data and information.

It would be a good idea to store that information – keep links as bookmarks, or use note-taking software, such as Evernote or OneNote, to record what you find and keep copies of web pages and relevant images. This will provide you with a data bank of material so that you can always see things from the perspective of the customer. Even if you cannot influence your company website, you can at the very least achieve this.

However, there is more you can do. You can trawl the information you gather for any errors or mistakes. Blog posts from previous buyers, for instance, may have some details about your products recorded incorrectly. Or reviews on ecommerce sites could be ill-informed. If you have the power to correct such things or add additional comments, then do so; otherwise, get your boss to organize this because potential customers could be put off buying unless you get the material corrected. In the UK Channel 5 television series *The Hotel Inspector* there is a recurring theme that the correction of previously negative reviews on travel websites leads to improvements in sales. It is an indication that information about your products or services on other websites impacts upon your sales.

If you can influence what your company does online, or even change it, then there are several things that can be done to connect the online and offline experiences. For instance, according to *Entrepreneur* magazine people expect to see your company phone number and physical address on every page of your website. Often, people are just visiting your website to find out where you are, how to get to you or what your number is so that they can call you and ask questions. One thing that many websites fail to do sufficiently well is to make those real-world connections.

For companies with sales teams it is also a good idea to have pictures and biographies of sales staff on the website. In that way, customers can start to build relationships with sales executives before they even meet them. If your sales team page also has email and social networking addresses for each of your staff, then customers can start an online relationship before they extend that in the real world.

Remember, too, that because people use websites to research products that they are going to buy in the real world, offline, they need plenty of information on the web pages they are looking at. In real-world selling there are generally several conversations between the buyer and the seller – other than in commodity purchasing such as groceries. For most sales, though, the sales person is involved in providing information to the buyer to help them make their purchasing decision. That means when people research online before buying they are seeking answers to the kinds of questions they would normally ask – they are looking for all the information they need to help them make their buying decision. This means that websites need to be completely and fully informative. Having a transaction-based site that merely gives a few product details and a means of ordering is not enough. Amazon, for instance, saw sales rise when it added reviews. ASOS, the leading online fashion store, saw sales increases when it added blogs and a magazine to provide even more information about its products. The more informative your website is about what you sell, the more likely your website is able to trigger purchasing.

Also, it is worthwhile considering what you can do using social media. Even if you do not have the option to alter the company's website you can still use social networks like LinkedIn or Facebook on a personal basis to connect with your customers and potential clients. Again, if you use these services to provide as much detailed information about what you are selling, you will increase the chances of people buying what you sell, even if they eventually buy offline.

You cannot ignore the online world when selling. Even if you do not sell much online directly to people, your web activity will help those offline sales. But if you ignore the importance of the web in terms of triggering sales, you will lose out to competitors who harness the power of the Internet.

So what are the big takeaways here?

- **The Internet is essential for sales:** The Internet is the starting point for almost everything that we sell.
- **The web is your customer's main research tool:** People research what they want to buy online; make sure you do the same research.
- **The Internet will continue to increase its importance:** The Internet will increasingly take sales away from the real world, raising its importance still further.

Source

www.bhengagement.com/report/2014-uk-shopper-behaviour-study

See also

Chapter 4 – Email sells more than the web

Chapter 15 – Buyers behave differently now

Chapter 17 – How to sell to silver surfers

Chapter 27 – Cold calls weaken sales

Further reading

Jones, Graham, *Click.ology: What Works In Online Shopping and How Your Business Can Use Consumer Psychology to Succeed* (Nicholas Brealey Publishing, London, 2014)

blog.earnest-agency.com/blog/2012/09/11/vital-statistics-for-b2b-marketers-two-inbound-vs-outbound

www.grahamjones.co.uk/2014/blog/retail/websites-dominate-shoppers.html

www.thinkwithgoogle.com/articles/five-ways-retail-has-changed-and-how-businesses-can-adapt.html

www.entrepreneur.com/article/207300

6 NICHES MAKE PROFITS

The Internet is making narrow categories more profitable

The Long Tail theory was an idea produced by the journalist Chris Anderson of *Wired* magazine in his analysis of the growing trend of ecommerce. The notion is that more sales are made from less popular items than from popular items. A way to imagine what this means is to consider sales of CDs. Even a large store such as Walmart cannot stock all the CDs currently available. Walmart stocks the Top 200. It does not have the shelf space to display the remaining few million CDs that are published. Neither can it cope with the logistics – if the customer wanting to buy a rare CD is in Chicago but the only copies of that item are in New York then no sale is going to be made. The Top 200 sells in every store – that's why they are the top CDs; they sell the most. However, The Long Tail theory shows this is not true.

If the Top 200 CDs sold, say, 1,000 copies per week, then the next 200 CDs must sell fewer copies, of course, say 800. The next group of CDs, those ending up in the Top 600 will sell fewer still, say 600 copies – and so on right down to the 4 millionth most popular CD in the world, which would probably only sell one copy a year. But as you can see, if you add the sales of the CDs in the charts between 200 and 600 you end up with 1,400 being sold, meaning that you have already outsold the Top 200. Imagine the total number of sales if you add together the CDs from position 201 to 4 million. That simply dwarfs the sales made by the Top 200.

The problem for a store like Walmart is shelf space and logistics. A typical Walmart store has fewer than 200,000 different product lines. Meanwhile Amazon has more than 230 million different product lines on sale. They can do that because there are no physical limitations on shelf space and no logistics issues.

It does not matter where that least popular CD is stored in the world because it can be posted to the one buyer a year who wants it.

What this has meant is that Amazon can exploit the 'long tail'. It can sell items that a typical retailer cannot sell due to shelf space and logistics limitations. Indeed, around 40 per cent of all Amazon's income comes from items that are, by definition, its least popular. Buyers have previously been limited to purchasing what was selected for them by the retailer. Even if a shopper wanted something different or more specialist, they couldn't get it because the shop only sold what they wanted to sell, not necessarily what the customers desired. Customers had to compromise. Now, though, with the advent of online shopping web retailers can sell everything that is available. That has meant a much wider variety of products being bought.

The Long Tail theory itself holds that it is the wider selection of products combined with online search facilities that has enabled several small niche markets to become established. People can make money now from small niches that previously would have been too expensive to operate. If you want, for instance, to buy fake moustaches there are now websites such as facetache.com that can sell you what you want, anywhere in the world, any time of the day or night. Prior to the Internet, selling such specialist items would have been unprofitable as the costs of the operation would have dramatically outweighed any sales available in one local area.

However, research suggests there is another reason why niche markets are encountering high levels of attention and that is embarrassment. A study conducted by Ryan C. McDevitt at the Simon Graduate School of Business of the University of Rochester, New York, USA, suggested that people may find it less embarrassing to buy rarer or less popular products online than they would in the real world. This is because of the degree to which the Internet can provide at least some anonymity. Even if you have to provide your name and address online, no one really knows you. Whereas if you were to buy the same products in a real world store you could be seen – perhaps identified or even spotted by a neighbour. This appears to limit our purchasing behaviour in the real world, making it more likely that we buy popular items, rather than the rarer, more specific items we might actually prefer.

This combination of the fear of embarrassment together with the wider availability of products and the ease with which we can find them using online search means that increasing amounts of sales are being generated from what would otherwise be rare or unpopular items. Indeed, the impact of the ease of finding these rare items has been demonstrated in research from the University of New York on mobile phones. This found that purchases tended to be more concentrated in the popular items, rather than in the whole extent of the Long Tail. This is thought to be because searching on a mobile for rare items is more cumbersome than when using a desktop computer. Consequently, people tend to stick with the well-established and popular items when shopping from a mobile phone. It demonstrates that it is the ease of finding rare items that is partly responsible for their sales.

This is an important finding for almost any business. Most companies have product offerings that can be tailor-made to specific and tiny niche markets. Even service-based businesses can target their sales to a multitude of niches. For instance, you could be selling accountancy services to local retailers which might bring in a certain level of sales. But if you then subdivided that into accountancy services for florist shops, accountancy services for butchers, accountancy services for bakers and so on you would be likely to attract more total business than if you targeted the more general retail sector. The four butchers in the town, for instance, would all want to have their accounts done by a butcher specialist, whereas none of them might want to have their accounts done by a generalist retail accountant. More overall business can be obtained by selling to multiple niche markets than can be achieved by generalizing. The same would be true for product sales. Imagine you sell candles. All kinds of people want candles. But if you sold candles to men looking for presents for their wife, to wedding planners, to funeral directors and so on, you would gain increased sales due to the perceived specialization of the candles. Yet the candles themselves could all be much the same.

This specialization into niches would not have worked prior to the Internet, but now your company can have a multitude of websites or 'landing pages' that demonstrate a niche within the Long Tail. It has become affordable to set up a variety of shops all targeting different niche markets. This leads to increased sales in the same way that Walmart might get increased CD sales if only it could stock the bottom four million instead of the Top 200.

In practical terms this means constantly looking for potential Long Tail niches. Ideas for these can come from the questions that are frequently asked by customers as well as from the website analytics that show the kind of search phrases used to reach your business website. When several people talk about a specialized version of your products or services and there is a reasonable number of people doing much the same when searching for you online, then it is time to consider setting up a specialist shop for that niche. With several such niches you can benefit from the Long Tail effect of building up multiple sales niches that collectively generate more cash than one generalized area of selling. Not only that, the popular end of the market is usually characterized by high competition, whereas niches that operate in the Long Tail tend to have very low numbers of competitors. This makes niche sales markets even more profitable.

It is also worth exploring whether you can create new product or service offerings for specific niches. Rather than wait for the website analytics to alert you to potential sales, you could create a whole new niche market. For example, you might sell curtains and you have several small offcuts left over each month. They might well be useful to sell to people who run toy theatres. There will only be a few thousand of those worldwide, but if someone specialized in their arena they would be likely to buy. Coming up with ideas for niches using your existing products or services is another approach to benefiting from the Long Tail.

So what are the big takeaways here?

- **Narrow niches are becoming more and more important:** Increasingly narrow niches for products and services lead to significant sales.

- **Divide your products and services into narrow niches:** Identify the niches which your products and services can be divided into.
- **Increased profits come from selling in multiple niches:** Selling in multiple niches can be more profitable than selling to a large single marketplace.

Sources

McDevitt, Ryan C. (2012), 'The Internet Lowers Inhibitions: Implications for the Long Tail', University of Rochester working paper

https://faculty.fuqua.duke.edu/~rcm26/mcdevitt_internet_inhibitions_april_2012.pdf

http://aisel.aisnet.org/icis2013/proceedings/ResearchInProgress/67

See also

Chapter 15 – Buyers behave differently now

Chapter 17 – How to sell to silver surfers

Chapter 22 – Upselling works through customer focus

Further reading

Anderson, Chris, *The Longer Long Tail: How Endless Choice is Creating Unlimited Demand* (Random House Business, New York, 2009)

7 MAKE TIME FOR MORE APPOINTMENTS

Be flexible in making short-term meeting arrangements

Sales appointments are still an important part of selling. Even though we have all sorts of ways of selling directly, such as using the Internet or even selling through mobile apps, sales appointments are still as popular as ever. Indeed, there are an estimated 498,000 people in sales jobs in London and the South East of England, according to *Metro* newspaper. If each of these people had just one appointment per day and if they only worked 48 weeks a year that's around 120 million sales appointments just happening in this part of the UK each year. Now, add up all those other parts of the country and allow for more than one appointment per day and you can see that each year in the UK alone there are going to be billions of sales appointments happening. Indeed, if you consider just shops, there are 1.5 m people involved in retail sales, all seeing several people per day. The chances are, there are literally thousands of sales appointments happening at this very moment. That's just in the UK. Now add up all the other nations in the world. In spite of the massive interest in online shopping, sales appointments are a significant and time-consuming activity for businesses.

The problem for sales people, however, is how they fit in all the appointments as well as write up their meeting notes, learn about new products, go to management meetings and catch up on all their emails. Time management is clearly an issue for sales people.

This factor was highlighted in a research study led by the University of Montpellier in France together with scientists from Indiana, Houston and Tennessee. This research looked at the way 249 sales executives from a TV broadcasting channel managed their time. These sales people were all involved in getting advertisers for the TV station. Like any other sales team they had targets to achieve and had to spend a great deal of time 'juggling' in order to get their work done. That is familiar territory for most sales people.

What the study revealed was that sales staff who had a tendency to 'polychronicity' were the better performers. People who are 'polychrons' are those who find it easy to run multiple tasks at the same time. This is not the same, necessarily, as multi-tasking, whereby people try to work on several tasks simultaneously. There is plenty of research that shows this lowers performance. But polychrons are people who manage to keep several things going at the same time and are able to switch between them with ease. The Montpellier study found that people who could do this managed their time better and had better sales performances than those who did not behave like this.

In addition, the researchers found that when sales staff were able to manage their own diaries and were not reliant on a manager to organize their time, they also performed better. The best sales people were those who ran their own diary and who could juggle all their work activities simultaneously.

Now, given that sales appointments are some of the most common and important activities in a sales person's diary, the research implies two things. First, it means that sales leaders need to provide more autonomy to sales staff so they can manage their own diaries. Second, it suggests that the employment of sales staff should include a measure of whether or not candidates are polychrons. If both of these things happen, the sales performances of the team will improve, at least according to the evidence from the French research.

This study is also backed up with evidence from research on car sales people in Canada. This found that when sales people who were motivated to achieve were also able to manage their time on a short-term basis, they were more successful. It seems, therefore, that when sales people have good time-management skills that allow them to focus on juggling lots of short-term tasks and when they are given the power to do this themselves, then that is when they are the most successful. The Canadian research adds to the French study and shows that focusing on short-term goals is more successful for sales people than concentrating on long-term targets. That is also a message for sales managers who may well improve the success of their sales teams if they provide weekly or monthly targets instead of annual ones. Sales people appear to perform better when the achievements they are seeking are in the near future instead of being distant. That also suggests that instead of focusing on how many sales appointments are needed in a month or a year, staff would do better if they are given weekly, perhaps even daily targets to achieve.

From a practical perspective for individual sales people these research studies imply that the best thing to do in terms of gaining sales appointments and making them a success is to focus on near-time appointments. Instead of looking for appointments next month, look for ones this week. However, to make that work you need to have a flexible polychron attitude, juggling all the new appointments as you make them. This might seem somewhat disorganized but the research confirms that dealing with things in the short term and juggling several of them at the same time is linked to increased sales performance.

The research did find that having modern time management tools, such as online CRM systems is a real help in organizing a sales person's time. Many firms have CRM systems already, but a lot of smaller businesses do not have such systems in place. With these applications the research shows that the juggling of time requirements is much easier. In other words, if you have a CRM system you provide your sales team with a tool that helps improve sales performance not just through the knowledge it provides, but also by enabling the users to manage their time more flexibly.

The French researchers pointed out in their discussion that sales people often find it difficult to estimate how long each item will take to complete. Sometimes people underestimate a task's complexity and do not give enough time in their schedule for it; on other occasions they think a task will take much longer than it does, meaning their diary has gaps in it that could be filled with useful productive selling.

This suggests that a key skill requirement for sales people is learning how to accurately estimate the time each of their tasks is likely to take. Then they can manage their diary in better ways, thus making them more efficient. One of the key issues in estimating time accurately is knowing how long each of the elements of the task will take. Often, people simply estimate the length of the whole task, without considering what you might call the 'sub-tasks'. So, the first step in good time estimation is to break down a task into the smaller sub-tasks that make up the whole thing.

For instance, you might need to write a report for your boss on the potential for sales in a new territory. You might estimate this will take you six hours to complete. But if you broke it down into 'online research about the territory', 'telephone research about the territory', 'thinking about the results of the research', 'deciding on the structure of the report' and 'writing the report' you would be able to more accurately estimate how long each of these tasks would be and realize that six hours was nowhere near enough...!

Another important method of estimating the time likely to be required is to keep a log of time actually spent. There are plenty of time-logging programs available for desktop computers or mobile devices that show exactly how much time you spent on particular activities. You can then look back at your past history and see how long particular tasks actually took, rather than guessing incorrectly and thereby managing your time poorly.

Most importantly, though, in terms of making enough time available for all those sales appointments, is having a flexible approach to time management and being able to focus only on the short term. Do that by estimating accurately the time each task will take and the research shows you will improve your sales performance.

So what are the big takeaways here?

- **Avoid focusing on the long term:** Short-term time management improves sales performance.

- **Flexibility is key:** Learn how to manage your time in a flexible way.
- **Get better at estimating time required:** Improve your ability to estimate the time each task takes and you will be able to manage your schedules better, enabling you to get more appointments.

Sources

Fournier, C., Weeks, W., Blocker, C. & Chonko, L. (2013), 'Polychronicity and Scheduling's Role in Reducing Role Stress and Enhancing Sales Performance', *Journal of Personal Selling & Sales Management*, Vol. 33 Issue 2 pp 197–210

www.metroclassified.co.uk/recruitment/recruitsales

www.baylor.edu/business/kellercenter/news.php?action=story&story=142981

See also

Chapter 8 – Getting past the gatekeepers

Chapter 10 – Networking works sometimes

Chapter 12 – How to find prospects

Further reading

Kahle, Dave, *11 Secrets Of Time Management For Salespeople: Gain the Competitive Edge and Make Every Second Count* (Career Press, New Jersey, 2013)

www.mindtools.com/pages/article/newPPM_01.htm

8 GETTING PAST THE GATEKEEPERS

Secretaries and PAs are willing to help you,
if you speak with them effectively

Gatekeepers are the barriers all sales people come up against every single day. The person you really want to speak with or make an appointment to see just does not answer their phone or even reply to the emails you send them. Instead, they employ a secretary or executive assistant who filters out the cold callers so that the boss only gets to hear about the people who are really worth seeing. Those gatekeepers are truly powerful individuals – they decide who will get a chance to pitch to the business. Fail their audition and you have no hope of getting inside the company to try to sell something.

So just how do you get past these gatekeepers so you can start selling? Thankfully Sam Williams, who runs a sales training company in Tucson, Arizona, interviewed several executive assistants in some research that found the key ways in which gatekeepers can become convinced to open up access to their boss.

The study found that almost all sales calls are blocked from getting anywhere near the boss. Indeed, the average number of sales people who make it through the gatekeeper is just 2 per cent, according to the executive assistants who were interviewed. Considering the research found that an average of 120 different sales calls are received each month that means only two or three people a month get to contact the boss directly – less than one a week. This means that the chances of actually getting past a gatekeeper are so slim it is a wonder that sales people keep on trying to achieve it.

The research, however, provides pointers to getting past those gatekeepers. The one thing that comes out of this qualitative study of executive assistants is that the successful sales people have already found out a great deal about the company they are approaching and they know exactly how they might benefit from what they are trying to sell. The interviewees also pointed out that calls from such well-prepared people need to be short – the gatekeepers are busy people too and do not want time-wasters.

The study also showed what not to do. One of the main ways whereby sales people become almost 'blacklisted' is to try to get around the barrier of the gatekeeper. The gatekeeper may have already put them off, so the sales person may well try to call someone else in the company, even saying that they have been recommended by the gatekeeper. Of course, those calls just go 'on hold' while the recipient checks whether or not this is true. If it isn't, the sales person is politely told 'no thank you' and from that moment on they are going to be ignored. Another negative for sales people is the poorly written sales letter. According to the executive assistants in the study most sales people cannot write a concise and clear letter. Indeed, the study found that the gatekeepers prefer phone calls to letters, but if letters are good – short and to the point – they stand out. One piece of advice from the gatekeepers was that if a sales person wants to write a letter it is probably worth a phone call first to ask what to put in writing. In other words, get advice from the gatekeeper on how to compose a letter that could lead to results.

That this small study of executive assistants found there was such a slim chance of getting through to the actual person you want to see should be a signal that getting it right is essential if your sales calls are to be successful. Crucial to that success is knowing as much about the company as possible, as well as knowing what they are likely to want and the benefits they could obtain from whatever it is you are trying to sell. This goes beyond the normal assumptions often made by sales people and implies detailed research in advance of the call.

Thankfully, the Internet means that there is a wealth of information available for sales people. Not only should you investigate the company's website, but it is also worthwhile checking your competitors to see the way they work and the kind of products and services they both sell and use.

One of the most important tools for sales people, however, is the social network LinkedIn. Not only does this provide a great deal of information about companies, but it also has extensive information on individuals within those businesses. This means that by carefully analysing what you can find on LinkedIn you can be much better prepared for the sales call. All you need to do is search for the company you are targeting and LinkedIn will present you with a list of the people who work there and who have profiles on the social network. You can then read through the relevant profiles and find out a wealth of information about these individuals and who works with whom. You can also find out how well connected you are to them; LinkedIn automatically tells you whether or not you are already connected or how many people it will take to reach these people. If someone, for instance, is a 2nd degree connection on LinkedIn it means you know someone who knows that individual. You can therefore contact your connection to find out what they know about the person you are targeting. In terms of being able to do your research about the people you want to target, there is probably no better online tool.

Of course, many businesses you may wish to target exist in the real world too. That's where actually visiting their shop, for instance, pays dividends because you can see their business in action and you can get a much better idea of the way they work and what they are likely to want from you. Mystery shopping in this way can provide plentiful information for a sales person. For service businesses with premises you cannot visit the situation is obviously more difficult, but you can mystery shop online, taking part in online chat if they have it, or sending an email for information.

Whichever way you go about it, though, the executive assistant research was clear – do your homework and go to them fully prepared and armed with plenty of information about the firm. Not knowing the name of the CEO, for instance, is a non-starter.

The research also revealed another important part of the homework you need to do: work out the return on the investment that you are asking them to make. Gatekeepers are only going to pass on sales information if it helps the company's bottom line. Therefore you need to work that out, or have a very good idea of the likely value to the company in terms of what you are selling.

Assuming you have both done all your homework and have the necessary information you still might not get past the gatekeeper. One hint provided in the study was that even a boss's family goes through the gatekeeper to reach them. Indeed, the gatekeeper becomes part of the family. In other words, these people are very close to the person you are trying to reach. That means if you want to get past the gatekeeper you are also going to have to be part of the family. This suggests getting to know the gatekeeper and their likes and dislikes. Get to know them as a person and build a relationship with them too. They are not just some kind of functionary designed to stop you getting in touch with the boss. They have all the same human emotions as the rest of us and that means they respond to kindness and having attention paid to them. Build a relationship with the gatekeeper and you stand a much greater chance of getting past them.

You are unlikely to get through to the person you want to speak to on your first phone call, so it is a good idea to use that call to start building a relationship with the gatekeeper. Ask them the best way to approach their boss, perhaps even what the best day or time would be. Then ask the gatekeeper what will help them, what you need to do to make it easy for them. In other words, start seeing this from their perspective and use your opening gambit to start building a relationship with them. One other thing the research reveals is to make those calls brief. You don't have to gather spurious details about their holiday…! But you do have to start to get to know them and be someone who is seen as supportive and helpful to them. You then significantly increase your chances of getting put through to the decision-maker.

So what are the big takeaways here?

- **Gatekeepers are your friends:** Build a good relationship with the gatekeeper to get to the boss.

- **Create a relationship with the gatekeeper:** Learn more about the companies you wish to approach and more about the gatekeepers themselves so you can talk to them as individuals not merely representatives of their firm.
- **Do your homework before speaking to a gatekeeper:** Gatekeepers say that sales people who have done their homework in advance and know the company in detail are the ones most likely to get an appointment.

Source

Sam Williams (2010), 'Should a sales person slip past the gatekeeper and the executive assistant to get to the boss?' *Inside Tucson Business*, Vol. 20 Issue 5 p 10

See also

Chapter 11 – Persistence pays in sales

Chapter 12 – How to find prospects

Chapter 18 – Get inside the mind of your buyer

Further reading

Muth, Dr Chuck, *Getting Past The Gatekeeper* (CreateSpace, 2014)

Stears, Anthony, *The Telephone Assassin* (Lulu.com, 2013)

9 KEY ACCOUNTS NEED KNOWLEDGE

*Information is key and needs sharing between
all sales team members*

Most business people know that you make more money from existing customers than you do from new customers. Yet, most businesses also spend much of their sales time trying to acquire new customers, rather than nurturing their existing clients. Indeed, according to the Pareto principle, 80 per cent of a company's income will come from just 20 per cent of its customers. Plus 80 per cent of that 20 per cent will be long-term customers who have been coming back year after year. If you look at your own company's data you'll almost certainly find that the most significant slice of your profits comes from the people who have been buying from you year after year after year.

Acquiring new customers is also expensive. It takes several sales calls or visits to get them to sign up to buying from you. Yet, getting an existing customer to buy something extra or to increase the size of their order often requires just a single phone call or email. The costs of getting more sales from existing clients are significantly higher than the costs of getting a new customer to buy just once. In other words, not only do you get more sales from existing customers, but those sales are more profitable.

Many businesses, though, are driven by fear. They are frightened that their existing customers will stop buying from them, so they spend ages trying to get new customers 'just in case'. Yet the main reason customers 'walk away' from their existing suppliers is that they feel neglected; they feel unloved and unwanted. If companies were to spend more time looking after the needs of their existing customers, they would be able to reduce their costs of customer acquisition as they would no longer be fearful of such clients leaving them.

This is the arena in which 'Key Account Management' plays a significant part. Managing key accounts – those accounts that bring you the most business – can be the principal way by which companies derive their profits. Managing those key accounts and strengthening the relationship between the business and its main customers means that they feel loved and wanted and therefore don't even consider walking away.

According to the Key Account Management expert Phil Jesson, the best way of ensuring that your customers stick with you is to view yourself as their business partner. Instead of seeing them as a customer and your business as a supplier, when your company has the view that it is in partnership with a client in a joint effort to improve their profitability, then it will also increase your own profits.

However, how do you go about managing such partnerships? This is an issue that was tackled by researchers in Finland when they investigated just how Key Account Management was implemented. The study involved an in-depth analysis of the work at Profi, an educational services firm, together with an in-depth review of literature on the subject. The researchers conducted several interviews with the staff at Profi as well as investigating their processes and systems. What came out of the research were several significant findings.

The most important was that Key Account Management only really succeeds if a company has an excellent ability to share knowledge. Although one or two people may be ultimately responsible for the relationship with a customer, everyone in the business needs to know about them. But equally the relationship managers need to know about everything within the business that could be important for their customers to know. In other words, the research implies that the key account manager is the linchpin between the company and the client, passing information between the two.

Another crucial finding in the Finnish research was that senior management were needed to provide support but that such help should not be 'top down'. Key account managers look to their bosses to provide clear guidelines and help when needed, but they also want to be independent and capable of thinking for themselves.

However, this could potentially conflict with another area of the research that looked at what you might call the 'ownership' of the customer. If the key account manager believes the customer is 'theirs' then that becomes an issue for knowledge sharing and transfer. If there is only one person in the business who can communicate with the customer that tends to make things work less well than might otherwise be the case.

This, though, brings up the issue of who should be the principal connection between the company and its key accounts. Should it be an expert in the products and services they buy, such as a product manager, or should it be someone who simply manages the key account? This was an issue raised in the Profi research – a concern that did not really get resolved. But it is a factor worth considering. If a product expert is the person responsible for managing a key account, this could provide them with a time conflict, especially if they have several customers to deal with. That would mean they would be spending less time on product-related issues. However, for the customer this is a good situation as it means the person they will be speaking with has the most knowledge and experience on the things they are interested in. But if that person simply does not have the time to manage the accounts, then a key account manager is usually appointed, who may well be excellent at personal relationship building, but may have insufficient product knowledge to satisfy the customer.

For this reason the key finding in the Finnish research was that the ability to share knowledge within an entire business is fundamental. It would mean, for instance, that a company could have two people who deal with a customer – a product expert and a relationship manager. But the effective and efficient sharing of knowledge means that the client would remain satisfied.

Quite how your business goes about sharing knowledge will depend upon several factors, such as the size of the firm, the kind of things your business sells and the types of customers you deal with. However, without some means of sharing knowledge from all sectors of your company you cannot hope to run key accounts effectively.

Many businesses simply have some kind of intranet, an internal set of web pages where files and documents are stored. That is not really knowledge sharing, though. That's the equivalent of putting a pile of documents in a room. Unless people go into that room and read through those documents, no knowledge is shared. Many firms operate under the illusion that by having an intranet they have shared knowledge.

Knowledge-sharing requires interaction. That means, perhaps, meetings or presentations, or online webinars, for example. It could also mean having some kind of internal social network, such as Yammer, to allow people to debate issues with each other. Knowledge-sharing also requires leadership, something which the Finnish research also revealed as being necessary. Key account managers wanted more guidelines and support from their bosses and leading knowledge-sharing is a clear role for such people.

Company bosses also have another role that will help knowledge-sharing and that is in fostering the right attitude. The potential pitfall of key accounts being seen as 'mine' by some sales staff clearly needs dissipating. Additionally, company leaders need to get the entire team believing that their role is to support their clients in the furtherance of those customers' profits.

The Finnish research was clear on one thing – sharing knowledge in a culture of supporting customers is the best way for a company to manage its key accounts. That means having the right attitudes and the right systems. But it also means employing the right kind of people to be key account managers. The Finnish researchers said that the best people to employ as key account managers are those who are professional and who also have the ability to have a wide understanding of the business, all its products and services. In other words, they need to retain a 'big picture' view of the firm as well as detailed knowledge. Considering people tend to be either 'big picture' individuals or 'details' people that's a tall order. Perhaps that is why it might be better to have two people running each key account – an expert, probably a detail person, and a manager, who looks at the big picture.

So what are the big takeaways here?

- **Share knowledge about customers:** Sharing knowledge is essential to keeping customers over the long term.
- **Set up a practical knowledge system:** Ensure your business has an adequate way of sharing knowledge that is usable and practical.
- **Share your knowledge with your customers:** You should view yourself as a business partner for your long-term clients with your aim being to help them become more profitable.

Source

Natti, S. and Palo, T. (2012), 'Key account management in business-to-business expert organisations: an exploratory study on the implementation process', *The Service Industries Journal*, Vol. 32 No. 11 August 2012, pp 1837–52

See also

Chapter 1 – Consultative selling is expected

Chapter 10 – Networking works sometimes

Chapter 18 – Get inside the mind of your buyer

Chapter 25 – Kindness kills objections

Chapter 39 – Customer knowledge depends on sales managers

Further reading

Jesson, Phil, *Piranhas in the Bidet: A Snappy Guide to Better Partnerships with Your Customers, Your People and Yourself!* (Author Essentials, 2014)

www.sellciusonline.com/2012/free-content/from-entertainer-to-business-partner-2.html

https://www.yammer.com

10 NETWORKING WORKS SOMETIMES

*Meeting up with existing clients can help
you get new business*

Business networking is one of those topics that many sales people shy away from. They often dislike having to go to some out-of-town hotel where a bunch of people who don't know each other gather to eat curled-up sandwiches and engage in small-talk before hearing someone read out aloud a bunch of PowerPoint® slides with all the enthusiasm of a pallbearer. Make no mistake: business networking events are not the most eagerly anticipated events of a sales person's year.

Yet they continue to take place with surprising regularity; there is bound to be a business networking event within 20 miles of your office within the next 24 hours. When you talk with people who go to these events, however, many moan about the same things. They complain about the lack of real prospects in the room, they say that the speaker was tedious and they question why they went in the first place. Yet, next month, they'll be back, hoping this time it will all be different.

People also complain about the 'business card hander' at networking events. This is the kind of individual who just goes from person to person, showing complete disinterest in them, merely handing out his business card saying something like 'well, if you ever need new stationery supplies, think of us'. Such people see business networking events as a way of finding new customers. Indeed, some people give up going to networking occasions because they did not gain any new business from their first three attempts.

At the same time, there are plenty of people who swear by networking, instead of at it. These people claim they can trace back new business they are doing to a networking event a couple of years ago, where they first met the individual who has now become a client, for instance. They see business networking as a 'long game' where instant results rarely happen.

So, for some businesses it appears that networking does work, yet for others it fails to produce the goods or is just seen as boring and time-wasting. Thankfully, research from Ulster University, Northern Ireland, has investigated the true impact of networking and how it can help businesses in a wide variety of ways. The research was conducted on owner-managed small businesses, but it is probably applicable to a wide variety of different kinds of firms because it also considers a large number of studies in drawing its conclusions. However, the researchers are keen to point out that the study may not be widely applicable unless it is repeated in other situations. Looking at the basis of the research, that is probably a cautious, though maybe scientifically correct conclusion. Talking with networking experts on the subject, it is pretty clear that the findings could be generalized to many business situations.

One of the key findings of the study is that business networking has a wide range of benefits. If businesses merely see a networking event as an occasion to try to make a sale, they are missing out on the many other potential benefits of such events. The study investigated the networking activities of 30 firms in Northern Ireland and was able to look in-depth at seven of these companies. The participating firms were from a variety of sectors, mostly B2B companies, though there were some which were B2C (business-to-consumer). This makes sense because consumers rarely attend business networking events, so they are predominantly for the business-to-business arena.

The research refused to include in its findings anything to do with business networking that only benefited one company; any benefits from business networking had to be shared by two or more companies for them to be considered in the research analysis.

Although the study found several significant benefits of networking, they largely fell into three main categories. The first is what you might call "filtering" – business networking allowed companies to filter out those people who were unlikely to ever buy from them. This is an important sales task, of course, because far too many sales people have conversations with people who are never going to buy from them. Business networking, it seems, is a very good way of qualifying likely clients, so time is not wasted on those who will not or cannot buy.

The second real benefit of networking is actually making sales. In spite of much advice found online on 'how to network', which concentrates on relationship building, this study found that one of the main benefits of attending business networks was actually making a sale.

A third – and potentially unexpected – finding of the research was that business networking was a good way of gaining information about competitors. This meant that those who went to business networking events were forewarned about what the competition was up to and could prepare their response. The research found this competitive information was particularly helpful in setting prices, since people at the networking events would often reveal what the competition was charging. Clearly, this is 'gold dust' information for anyone in sales.

These three main benefits of business networking are not, however, about making an 'instant sale'. Hence if you go to business events merely to get a customer there and then, you are missing out on being able to develop relationships that then go on to become customers and who will provide you with detailed information on your competitors. The people who think that business networking is a 'long game' appear to be right.

Another finding of this research was also about those long-term relationships. It appears that businesses benefited from attending networking events so they could meet existing customers. One of the key reasons for going to business networking meetings for some of the people in the study was to be able to maintain a relationship so they could gain future, repeat business. Some of the businesses in the study also used networking to keep up to date with the activities of their existing customers so they could determine whether or not future business was likely or unlikely. By discovering that an existing client had budgetary issues, for instance, it means that plans can be made to counteract the likely drop in sales from them. Clearly this is really all part of good key account management.

What the networking research implies is that from a practical sales perspective it is a good idea to go to a networking event with a client. Rather than going to meet someone, or in the hope that a client will be there, it seems that if you can agree to attend together it will benefit your sales by allowing you to find out more information about the customer as well as to strengthen the relationship. Going to networking events on your own, in the hope that you might meet someone who you could sell something to, appears to be a waste of time. But going to a networking event together with an existing client has potential benefits for both of you. Not only does it help cement relationships, but by both being there you can help each other with information about your respective competitors.

Considering that the study also found that business networking events are a good place for research, whether it is on competitors, existing clients or qualifying prospects, it is a good idea to have some means of recording your findings. Whether that is a notebook or some database system is bound to be down to a combination of personal preferences and company requirements. However, most likely you will have a smartphone and you could use that to quickly voice-record your thoughts and findings at the end of the evening for later transcribing into your company's knowledge system. Alternatively, you could use an app, such as Evernote, to record details of your findings at a business networking event and store them in an electronic notebook for each customer or prospect. Either way, having some means of recording what happened at the event is a good idea.

One other clearly important practical aspect of going to a business networking event is to try to get hold of an attendee list in advance. Many events these days are organized using some kind of online registration system and these frequently provide a list of people who have signed up. Knowing who will be there means that you can plan in advance who you want to speak with and what you want to talk to them about. It may be qualifying them as a potential prospect, or as a company to forget, or it might be to seek out competitor information. But going to a networking event with some kind of mini-plan as to what you want to achieve will help ensure you make the most of the benefits discovered by the research in Northern Ireland.

So what are the big takeaways here?

- **Do not network to find new clients:** Networking with existing clients can be more fruitful than networking with potential new clients.
- **Plan your networking events:** Schedule as many opportunities as possible to meet existing clients at networking events.
- **Networking is a way of increasing competitor knowledge:** Networking isn't always about immediate sales – it can be about acquiring competitive knowledge that helps protect future sales.

Source

O'Donnell, A. (2014), 'The Contribution of Networking to Small Firm Marketing', *Journal of Small Business Management* Vol. 52 Issue 1 pp 164–87

See also

Chapter 9 – Key accounts need knowledge

Chapter 12 – How to find prospects

Chapter 13 – Referral sales are worth having

Chapter 28 – Perfect pitches come from mood setting

Further reading

Kintish, Will, *Business Networking – The Survival Guide: How to make networking less about stress and more about success* (Pearson, London, 2014)

11 **PERSISTENCE PAYS IN SALES**

Most sales are made after the fifth call, so don't stop phoning

How many calls do you make to someone who is a potential customer before you give up calling them? If you are like most sales people you give up too soon. We all tend to give up early because we fear that we are annoying the prospect. We tend to believe that if we called them one more time, they'll become angry or negative in some way. So we 'cool it' and decide to stop making those calls. Then, we forget the prospect because after several months we have moved on. So have they. There is also another reason why sales people give up calling – and it's a reason that sales managers complain about. Like it or not, some sales people are just plain lazy. They give up calling potential customers because it is just too much bother to keep on calling.

Dartnell Corp did some analysis of sales call performance and discovered that 80 per cent of all purchases are made after the fifth phone call. At the same time, though, 48 per cent of sales people only make a single call to prospects. A further 25 per cent give up after making a second call. By the time the fifth call is being made – the one where most purchases will take place – only 10 per cent of sales people are bothering to make calls. It turns out that 80 per cent of all purchases are made to just 10 per cent of sales people – the ones who did not give up calling. Nine out of ten sales people give up before 80 per cent of sales will be made.

A similar analysis by the sales expert Jeffrey Gitomer found that it took seven 'no thank you' answers before a purchase was made. Together with the findings from Dartnell it confirms that most sales are won by the most persistent sales people. It also probably helps if you have a pretty thick skin and can therefore brush off rejection after rejection after rejection.

Sales managers know that in each team they have someone who brings in a significant slice of the sales. That individual's colleagues wonder how they do it. The research suggests it is simply never giving up. That doesn't mean staying on the phone until you get a sale; that would be 'badgering' people into a purchase. Instead it means that these highly successful sales people make regular appointments to call on their prospects until they do get a sale.

If you consider this from the perspective of the prospect it might seem as though the repetitive calls are a nuisance and could be annoying. But that's not the case. Research conducted in Spain over a two-year period found that the frequency of sales calls was related to perceived value and a higher level of customer service. In other words, the more calls you make, the more the customer likes you and your company. Far from being seen as a nuisance, the repeated phone calls are seen more positively than the occasional call.

This makes sense from a basic psychological perspective. Imagine you are dating someone for the first time. You have a great evening and you decide another date is worthwhile. So you call again and your prospective partner is not so sure. So you give up. But all that date is really doing is testing you – they are trying to find out the true extent of your interest. If you are truly interested in them, you will call again. If you do not, then they know the second date was a bad idea. In a similar way, it seems sales prospects like it if we keep calling.

The Spanish research investigated the sales activity of 357 different sales prospects. They monitored what was happening over a period of two years in order to gain a long-term insight into the effectiveness of the sales call process. The study included an experimental element where a control group of customers was given the usual number of sales calls. However, in another group the rate of calling was increased. This enabled the researchers to see if there was any impact from increased frequency of calling. The customers in each of the two groups were matched so that there was little impact due to the size or nature of their businesses.

The study discovered that a simple increase in calling rate led to an 18 per cent rise in sales over the two-year period of the research. In other words, additional sales calls led to increased sales volumes. The customers also reported a 22 per cent increase in satisfaction with their supplier and 10 per cent rise in perceived value for money. In other words, just making more calls to their customers led to several increases in positive feelings about the company. Interestingly, the research found no significant relationship between perceived value for money and the length of any relationship between the client and the company. The other measures, such as satisfaction, were linked to how long the two parties had known each other. What this suggests is that an increased frequency of calling is not seen as annoying by people who hardly know you. Instead, they appear to think they are getting a good deal.

An interesting aspect of the study was that the higher up the level of authority the individual customer was, the more they liked an increased number of phone calls. In other words, contrary to popular belief and assumption, the more senior a customer or prospect, the more they prefer additional phone calls. In many sales people there is a tendency to want to call the senior figures less frequently, because they are 'busy' or 'too important' for their call. This research suggests that this notion can be forgotten because there was a greater level of satisfaction from the senior people who were called more frequently.

In practical terms, these findings, together with the data from Dartnell, suggest that sales people need to, first, reconsider their assumptions and check their fears. Far from annoying customers and prospects, additional sales calls appear to make them warm to you rather than get angry. Furthermore, the higher up the prospect is within the hierarchy of their company, the more they want you to call more often. So, set aside your fears – they are imaginary.

However, it is also important not to come across as 'pushy', so a significant element in making sure that your customers feel good about you is to timetable your calls so they are frequent, but not overbearing. This means having an efficient diary system, perhaps embedded within a CRM system. In that way you can record the details of the latest call and then plan and schedule your next call at an appropriate time. This is also where you can use gatekeeper knowledge as they will tell you what is the best day and time to make your call. If you do not become systematic in your sales calls, though, you will forget to have the follow-up conversations and that will result in your customers thinking more negatively about you.

For sales managers, this research also suggests that they should allow more time for sales people to make calls. Instead of counting sales, it might be more appropriate to count calls. How many times does each sales person call prospects and clients? Targets along those lines might be more helpful because those additional calls will lead to more sales, according to this Spanish research study.

One other important practical aspect that needs considering is that the Spanish research found that face-to-face contact prior to the phone calls was preferable and was linked to better results. That would suggest that prospecting in 'real world' situations, such as exhibitions or business networking events, is a good place to start, following up such face-to-face meetings with a series of phone calls. In other words, the research implies that sales managers need to consider their entire prospecting and follow-up systems, with initial face-to-face meetings giving way to phone calls and emails later.

Even if you cannot achieve that, though, the research is pretty conclusive: persistence pays.

So what are the big takeaways here?

- **Do not give up too soon:** Most sales are made after the fifth call to a prospect; yet most sales people give up after the second call.
- **Track your sales calls:** Develop a persistent attitude and ensure you have a means of tracking calls made and making diary entries for future calls.
- **Avoid showing you do not like customers:** Potential customers think you are not interested in them if you give up calling them.

Sources

Roman, S., Martin, P. (2008), 'Changes in sales call frequency: A longitudinal examination of the consequences in the supplier–customer relationship', *Industrial Marketing Management* Vol. 37 Issue 5 pp 554–64

www.dartnellcorp.com

See also

Chapter 12 – How to find prospects

Chapter 18 – Get inside the mind of your buyer

Chapter 27 – Cold calls weaken sales

Further reading

Gitomer, Jeffrey, *The Sales Bible: The Ultimate Sales Resource* (Wiley, New Jersey, 2003)

www.eyesonsales.com/content/article/know_when_to_quit_but_dont_quit_too_soon_rcpcat

12 HOW TO FIND PROSPECTS

*Qualifying who is likely to buy is the only
way to find real prospects*

According to the business growth expert Roger Harrop, getting
more sales is directly related to the amount of prospecting a
company does. He says it is purely a numbers game – contact
more people and you will make more sales. Interestingly, though,
a study conducted in 2010 by the leadership training company
Achieve Global found that even the most ardent supporters of
doing lots of prospecting only spent eight hours a week on it.
Most individuals in their study of 300 sales people spent less than
four hours a week on finding new prospects. The sales people in
the study cited lack of time, lack of motivation and an inability
to source leads in the first place as their reasons for not doing
more prospecting.

Perhaps part of the reason for this is revealed in the Achieve
Global study, which went on to research the 56 sales managers
responsible for the sales teams. These managers were asked to
rank sales prospecting activities in order of importance. They
found it difficult to distinguish between 13 different elements
of prospecting, saying largely that almost all of them were of
equal priority. However, they marginally ranked what you might
call 'administrative' tasks as more important than the tactical
activities in making the sale. Things like prioritizing, planning
and tracking were put higher up the list of priorities than how
to leave an effective voicemail or how to overcome indifference.
In other words, it appears that sales people could well be put
off prospecting because their managers are turning it into an
activity that is admin heavy. This is further emphasized by the
sales managers' future plans for training, which placed the most
importance on planning, well above practical techniques. You
have to ask yourself how can sales teams make more calls and get
more business if their time is spent on administrative tasks and

their focus, driven by their managers, is based on planning and prioritizing, instead of on more practical aspects.

To work out just how sales teams can improve their performance in prospecting you have to go back to research that was conducted in 1986. This research looked at the impact of 'prenotification' in sales calls. In other words, it investigated the notion that you called up a likely purchaser merely to tell them that you will be making a sales call to them in the future, or that you will be mailing them some interesting literature. The study was conducted by the University of Maryland and included an analysis of the prenotification technique as used by a burglar alarm company on almost 3,200 sales prospects.

Half of the prospects were met and a standard sales pitch took place. The other half had a prenotification telephone call and were then sent some literature in the post before the real sales call took place. The results were starkly different. Of the 1,563 prospects who were offered a sales meeting, only 96 took up the offer and of them only 7 actually bought anything. But of the 1,620 people given a prenotification telephone call, 226 agreed to the follow-up and of them 39 bought something. In percentage terms, the prenotification group bought twice as much as the traditional group.

Clearly from this research it is a 'numbers game' when it comes to prospecting, but you can increase those numbers using the simple technique of warning people in advance you are going to sell to them. That appears to make them more receptive when the sales call subsequently takes place. But how do you find enough numbers of likely buyers in the first place? That was dealt with in a further analysis of prospecting conducted by the University of Maryland more than a decade after its original research. This analysis found that most of a sales person's time spent on prospecting is dedicated to dealing with people who are never going to buy from them. As such these are not really prospects at all; they are 'suspects' – people who the sales executive has a hunch might buy, but nothing more than that.

This finding ties in with the Achieve Global study, which found that sales people find it hard to locate good, worthwhile leads. Perhaps the prenotification technique investigated by the

University of Maryland is merely a means of finding out who among the 'suspects' is an actual 'prospect'.

Crucially, the Maryland review suggests that real prospects are only worthwhile pinpointing if they satisfy three criteria:

1. They have a need that will be met by what you are trying to sell them
2. They have the ability to sign the cheque
3. They are receptive to having contact with you.

If they don't fit all three of these criteria, say the Maryland researchers, they are not prospects. Yet, in spite of this rather common-sense approach, it seems that sales people continue to call on people who have no need for their products, no means of paying for them and do not want to hear from them in the first place.

The analysis goes on to point out that there are also only three ways you can find these prospects: from within your company, from referrals and by doing it yourself. Referrals and leads from within your own company are much more likely to be good prospects. So it would seem that sales people are wasting a lot of time on calling or meeting people who are mere suspects and that most of these people are those they have found themselves. In other words, it suggests that far from not having the time to do more prospecting, the real issue with many sales people is not being able to spot the most likely buyers in the first place.

Often, sales people will know that the target has a need, but the crucial question identified by the Maryland research is 'does that person have the money and the authority to spend it?' If the person the sales person has identified as a likely buyer doesn't have the cash or the ability to authorize payments, it is a waste of time speaking with them. As a result, one of the most important things sales people can do in order to improve the results of their prospecting is to better identify those with budgets and spending power and who are also receptive to sales calls. This may well be where the prenotification works – it helps sales people get a better idea of who the prospects are from the suspects.

In practical terms the research suggests that sales people need to spend more time on prospecting generally. Simply making regular appointments in your diary to call more people will result in increased sales. However, you increase the chance of gaining those sales if you filter out the people who have no spending authority. Furthermore, by doing this you overcome one of the other problems with prospecting, the demotivating issue of getting so many rejections. One of the key difficulties for sales people as identified by Achieve Global was the lack of motivation to do any prospecting. Your motivation is bound to be improved if your strike rate is higher. The conversion rate you get from sales calls is higher if you prenotify, so it makes sense to spend some of your prospecting time asking people if you can call them later, sending out information in the post or through email and then following up on that at a later date. That process appears to filter out the suspects, allowing you to concentrate on the prospects that are more likely to buy.

So what are the big takeaways here?

- **Qualification makes people prospects:** Prospects are not really anything more than suspects unless you qualify them first.
- **Tell your prospects you are going to call them:** Find your suspects and prenotify them to increase the chances of turning a suspect into a prospect.
- **Establish a sales pathway to convert prospects:** Sales leads are everywhere. What is important is turning those possible buyers into actual buyers through a carefully planned pathway.

Sources

Jolson, M. A. (1986), 'Prospecting by Telephone Prenotification: An Application of the Foot-In-The-Door Technique', *Journal of Personal Selling & Sales Management*, Vol. 6 Issue 2 pp 39–42

Jolson, M. A. & Wotruba, T. (1992), 'Selling and Sales Management in Action: Prospecting: A New Look at this Old Challenge', *Journal of Personal Selling & Sales Management*, Vol. 12 Issue 4 pp 59–66

See also

Chapter 8 – Getting past the gatekeepers

Chapter 25 – Kindness kills objections

Chapter 27 – Cold calls weaken sales

Further reading

Harrop, Roger, *Win! How to succeed in the new game of business* (SRA Books, 2014)

Hopkins, Tom, *Sales Prospecting for Dummies* (John Wiley & Sons, New York, 1998)

www.achieveglobal.com/research-and-resources/research-documents.aspx

13 REFERRAL SALES ARE WORTH HAVING

*Most recommendations will come from
your least loyal customers*

Ask most business owners where they get the majority of their sales from and they will generally use one word – 'referrals'. This is 'word-of-mouth' marketing at its best, when someone recommends your services or products and you get a customer as a result. Indeed, sales leads from referrals are among the 'hottest' leads you can get. Someone else has identified they have a need and that your business can satisfy it. Furthermore, people do not recommend that their friends or colleagues buy something if they know they cannot afford it. As such, referrals are generally well-qualified prospects.

However, word of mouth marketing is only of real value if it leads to sales. Many businesses generate positive word of mouth that does not result in sales being made. Instead all it creates is a nice fuzzy feeling about the business – which is great, but does not help the bank balance. Thankfully, research conducted at Harvard University and at Yale University in 2004 discovered what it takes to make word-of-mouth marketing lead to those positive referrals.

The research looked at a marketing agency, called BzzAgent, and a restaurant chain, Rock Bottom Restaurant & Brewery. The study involved a 13-week field test in which 'real world' word of mouth was tested, as well as an online campaign to generate referrals. The aim of the study was to answer two main questions:

1. What kind of word of mouth matters most?
2. Who creates the word of mouth that matters?

The results are surprising, in one sense, in that the word of mouth that was produced by the less loyal customers was that which had the greatest impact. In another sense, of course, this is quite likely. Loyal customers are most probably buying repeatedly as a matter of course and not actually considering telling other people about you. To them it is rather 'routine', whereas to a new customer who has yet to become loyal, they are more likely to want to tell others about their 'brilliant new find'.

The research found that the most impact from word of mouth was between people who did not have strong ties to each other, such as acquaintances. Again, this is counterintuitive. You might think that the best recommendations come from the people we know best, such as friends or relatives. But the study showed that it was people with weak social ties that led to the most impact on referrals. This also makes sense because the people we have the strongest ties to are those we already know a lot about and therefore have probably heard them go on and on about their favourite products or services. Furthermore, if we know them well and we like the things they like, they are already 'preaching to the converted'. It is people we know less well who recommend things that get noticed by us.

The Harvard and Yale researchers then went on to run an experiment in a controlled setting to see if their field tests with the marketing agency and restaurant chain were likely to be correct. This experiment involved several students recommending websites to each other from a specific predetermined selection of sites. The students recruited their own friends to join the experiment so that the researchers had a pre-set selection of individuals who were more closely related to each other. The results of the experiment produced the same findings as the field test. What was clear was that recommendations to visit a website had most impact on people with the weak social ties. In other words, the people who hardly knew each other took more notice of one another's recommendations; the experiment had found precisely the same results as the field test with businesses.

The researchers were clear about what their findings meant. They said that if you want an effective word-of-mouth campaign you need to recruit your least loyal customers to do it for you. Recommendations from them will produce more sales. This is counterintuitive; indeed much advice on social media marketing on the Internet, for instance, is that you need to get opinion leaders and those with plenty of good deep relationships to recommend your products and services. The problem is, recommendations in this way produce fewer sales than if you use people who are weakly tied to each other and who also haven't bought much from you.

So how do you go about getting recommendations and referrals from people who haven't been a long-term customer? After all, it seems more logical that you could get more referrals from long-standing customers whom you have a good relationship with.

One answer to this is to systematize it. If your sales process has some kind of system in place for getting those referrals and recommendations you can use this to generate them from new customers. For instance, as soon as someone has bought online you can give them the facility to Tweet about it or add something to their Facebook timeline. If you run a B2B service you can provide new customers with postcards, for instance, to hand out at networking events. Or, if you are a retailer you could offer some kind of reward for new customers, perhaps along the lines of a discount voucher if they get five people into your store that day.

Of course, you do not just need to get referrals and recommendations from new customers. You can get them from existing customers, though the research points out you need to be selective and only choose the less loyal ones. So, one thing you can do to boost your sales through referrals is to use your CRM system or sales database to find people who only order rarely, or who haven't done so in quite a while. With this sub-set of customers at your fingertips you can then contact them and encourage them to recommend you. Naturally, you may need some kind of incentive for them to do this. You might therefore be able to make a sales call to these individuals and offer them some kind of deal, providing they do some recommending for you. Not only would you get additional sales through their word of mouth, but you may be able to sell something extra to them too.

Although it seems strange, it is also a good idea to avoid using opinion leaders to try to refer people to you. As the research from Harvard and Yale demonstrated, even though their recommendations and referrals will be seen by plenty of people, the impact such referrals have can be significantly lower than from your less well connected and less loyal customers. Hence, one thing to avoid is the temptation to focus on opinion leaders or people with a large fan base of some kind. It may well do your corporate ego some good by having these well-known and respected figures recommending you, but the impact on sales is going to be much less than if you get more unknown people to make the recommendations.

One other thing worth considering, however, is whether or not referrals are what you need. In spite of many businesses saying how important they are, there are certain arenas where referrals are probably not a good idea. For instance, products where the decision to buy is not important, such as something really cheap, are unlikely to warrant referrals and recommendations. Equally, services which are entirely subjective are unlikely to benefit from any kind of recommendation or referral system. So you have to be sure that if you are going to implement a referral system it has to be appropriate to your products or services.

So what are the big takeaways here?

- **Loyal customers are not much help:** Less loyal customers create the greatest referrals.
- **Focus on your least loyal customers:** Analyse your customer loyalty and get the ones who are least loyal to refer you, mention you, or write about you on social media.
- **Word of mouth from opinion leaders doesn't help much:** Opinion leaders are not the best people to help you create word-of-mouth referrals.

Source

Godes, D. & Mayzlin, D. (2009), 'Firm-Created Word-of-Mouth Communication: Evidence from a Field Test', *Marketing Science*, Vol. 28 Issue 4 pp 721–39

See also

Chapter 10 – Networking works sometimes

Chapter 12 – How to find prospects

Chapter 17 – How to sell to silver surfers

Chapter 28 – Perfect pitches come from mood setting

Further reading

Lopata, Andy, *Recommended: How to sell through networking and referrals* (Pearson Education, Harlow, 2011)

Silverman, George, *The Secrets of Word-of-Mouth Marketing* (American Management Association, New York, 2001)

14 AVOID TOO MUCH EYE CONTACT WITH CUSTOMERS

To get people to buy, don't look them in the eye

You'll never make a sale unless you look your customer in the eye – at least that's what they tell you on most sales training courses. Selling, of course, is about persuasion. As a sales person you are trying to persuade your potential customer that they really ought to buy your product. Sometimes that persuasion is easier than at other times, because the customer is more than halfway there to making that decision themselves. A lot of the time, though, a sales person is up against an individual who is not convinced that they need to buy. Your job in selling is to persuade them to change their minds.

The psychology of persuasions is a well-researched topic, but it is only recently that scientists have begun to look at some of the finer details of our persuasive behaviour. Researchers at the University of Freiburg in Germany conducted two key experiments in 2013, which demonstrated that there is indeed a relationship between eye contact and persuasiveness. But it is not the connection that most sales training courses teach.

The study found that the more someone was looked in the eye, the less likely they were to being persuaded to change their mind. Also, because this study was conducted using computerized video, it has implications for Internet-based sales, as well as face-to-face ones.

The first experiment involved participants watching two kinds of videos. In the first the person talking was looking directly into the camera, effectively making direct eye contact with the viewer. The second video had the speaker at an angle to the camera – their eyes could be seen, but they were not looking directly at the viewer. The participants completed a questionnaire about their beliefs and attitudes on the topics of the videos, before and after viewing them. During the time they watched the video, eye-tracking technology was able to determine what the participants were looking at on the screen. The results were clear: people who already agreed with what the video was about made the most eye contact with the speaker. However, there was also a relationship between attitudes and eye contact. The more eye contact people made, the less likely they were to change their attitudes. It seemed that the more eye contact, the less persuadable people became.

The second study involved participants watching two sets of videos – one where the speaker was in agreement with the viewer in terms of attitudes and another where they disagreed. In addition to watching these videos the groups of participants were broken into two groups. One group was asked to look directly into the eyes of the speaker on the video. The other group was instructed to only look at the speaker's mouth. This experiment found that people were more likely to have their attitude changed when they looked at the speaker's mouth rather than when they looked at the eyes. This was not related to prior agreement with what the speaker was saying.

Taken together, these experiments suggest that we tend to become less agreeable to persuasion when we look someone in the eye. That is the complete reverse of what most sales training courses teach. However, the German researchers mention that there are plenty of studies that point out the value of eye contact. For instance, research shows that eye contact is seen as something that is associated with trust. You are hardly likely to trust a sales person who does not make eye contact with you. Similarly, eye contact is associated with what is known as 'affiliative behaviour', which essentially means supporting each other and building a relationship with one another.

As a result, it is clear that eye contact can play a part in good sales behaviour. But this new research from Freiburg would suggest that there are also times when you do not want to make too much eye contact. At the crucial time when you want to persuade a potential customer to buy, this research suggests that is the precise time to look away. If you want to persuade someone to buy from you, then you need to make eye contact to build up a relationship and to gain the buyer's trust. But when it comes to those crucial moments when you need them to change their mind from non-buyer to buyer, then that is the time to look somewhere else – even if the prospect is looking at you in the eye.

From a practical perspective this is a real problem. If a sales person spends much of their time in front of people worrying about what they are looking at or where to look, their mind will become distracted from the conversation, potentially missing out on sales opportunities or being able to relate well to the customer. Furthermore, the customer will know that the sales person is not really concentrating and this will reduce trust and that all-important 'connection' between the two people.

It is clearly good to look at people in the eye when you want to relate to them well, but not so good when you want to persuade them to change their mind. So what can you do about this if you do not want to constantly have to think about eye contact? The simplest solution to this is to forget everything you have been told about eye contact…! In other words, treat the encounter as a normal social conversation. Let your instincts take over.

When you were developing as a small child you learned about the appropriate body language and non-verbal signals to accompany what you were saying. Most of the time you do not have to think about body language or eye contact. When you do, it all starts to go wrong because you are no longer behaving naturally. You instinctively know what kind of body language or eye contact to use based on the years of experience of human communication that you have had since a baby. You learned a vocal language as you grew up and so too you learned a non-vocal language. Rely on it. In sales encounters, avoid thinking about where to look too much and focus instead on having a normal human conversation. That way there is a great chance that you will reduce eye contact at precisely the right moment. When you were negotiating with mum and dad as a small child to get your own way, you will have learned that looking away helped. That is still inside your head – so use it, by being natural.

Where this German research really comes into its own is in the world of online sales communication. Many businesses now produce videos for channels such as YouTube in order to pitch their products and services. Frequently these are 'talking head' videos where someone sits facing the camera talking directly to the viewer. But as the German research showed, such videos are less persuasive than videos where the speaker is not looking at the camera. Hence, the best way to produce persuasive online sales videos is to use the interview format. This is where someone is almost side-on to the viewer, apparently talking to someone just 'off camera'. It is the typical kind of scenario when people are interviewed on television. The reporter is at the side of the camera and the interviewee looks at them, not the camera. This kind of video encounter is something we are all used to, plus the German research showed that people were more persuaded by people who did not look them in the eye on screen.

What this means is recording online sales videos either as interviews, or if that is not possible as though they were interviews, with the speaker facing an imaginary interviewer, just off camera is preferred. In this way your online videos will lead to more sales since what you say in these videos will become more likely to persuade people.

Having said that, the German research did find that eye contact was good for the people who already believe in what you are saying. This therefore implies you need two kinds of online video – one for the people who haven't made their mind up to buy and one for the customers who have their credit card already in their hand…! The second group of people are those who want and need eye contact from online video. It is therefore important to know what kind of people are going to particular pages on your website or to specific videos on YouTube. You need to direct the person who has yet to make up their mind to the interview-style video, whereas those who already know they want to buy from you, but just need some details confirmed, need to land on a page with a video that looks them in the eyes.

So what are the big takeaways here?

- **Avoid eye contact to increase sales:** Looking at people directly in the eye makes it less likely you will change their opinion from not wanting to buy something to agreeing to buy it.
- **Look all around you:** Look at eyes only occasionally; look around the face and surroundings – in other words behave naturally.
- **Just be yourself when it comes to body language:** Eye contact is natural, so don't avoid it completely. Equally, don't stare people in the eyes – you will decrease sales if you do.

Source

Chen, F. S. & Minson, J. A. (2013), 'In the Eye of the Beholder: Eye Contact Increases Resistance to Persuasion', *Psychological Science*, November Vol. 24 No. 11, pp 2254–61

See also

Chapter 16 – Selling to men or women is not the same

Chapter 17 – How to sell to silver surfers

Chapter 19 – Spotting those buying signals

Further reading

Ellsberg, Michael, *The Power of Eye Contact: Your Secret for Success in Business, Love, and Life* (William Morrow Paperbacks, New York, 2010)

15 BUYERS BEHAVE DIFFERENTLY NOW

*Customers spend more time researching
what they want than ever before*

There is little doubt that we all behave somewhat differently as
a result of the Internet. As was discussed in Chapter 5, most of
our sales journeys these days start online. But it is not just where
we discover products to buy, but the whole process of how we
purchase them that has changed in a relatively short amount
of time since the first online transactions. Google completed a
significant study into how people research and then buy products
and services that revealed a shift in our behaviour to a more
cautious approach to buying.

The research was conducted in 2011 and involved analysis of the
'clickstream' of 48,944 people. These were all individuals who
were panellists on research programmes conducted by Nielsen,
one of the world's largest consumer research companies. Google
tracked where these people clicked over a period of three months
in several different sectors, including travel, fashion, mobile
phones, insurance and property.

Google's study discovered that people take a long time to do their
research. Far from going online to find something to buy and
getting it there and then, the average time from the first click to
the actual purchase was 24 days. Strangely, some items that you
would think would have a long research time, such as financial
services, tended to have the shortest amount of research. More
than half (54 per cent) of people seeking information on energy
prices made their purchases within 24 hours. At the other end of
the research spectrum, however, were general retail purchases,
where a third of all items were bought after more than 30 days of

research. For travel, a quarter of purchases took place more than 30 days after the initial search was started.

For almost all the different sectors studied by Google the total number of purchases made didn't occur until 80 days or more after the individuals first started looking. In other words, for many items that people want to buy they are taking a very long time to research things to make sure that they are getting precisely what they want.

Google's research also looked at how many hours people spent on researching what they wanted to buy. The study found that the amount of time spent on research was often quite considerable – over three hours for items of fashion, for instance. Yet for financial items like loans, it was less than half an hour. What was also interesting was the number of different websites visited as people researched what they wanted to buy. On average, people visited 9.9 different websites, with loans, once again, having the lowest number of different sites visited. However, it was not just the number of different sites visited that was interesting, but how many times people kept returning to the same websites. Typically, they went back to the websites two or three times, with fashion being the highest for return visits at an average of 3.9 times.

Another element of the research was to look at how many different searches people conducted prior to their final selection. On average, people conducted seven searches, with travel getting the highest number of searches at 20 different terms being used. Importantly, other than mobile phones and car insurance, most of the time people were not searching for brands, but using more generic terms in their search phrases.

For a sales person this might all sound rather negative. The more websites people visit, the less they use your brand name and the longer they take to complete the research means it is all the more likely they will meet the competition. However, Google's study had one other interesting finding – the shopping baskets of the people who took these long periods of intensive research were on average 8 per cent higher than those who didn't do so much investigation. In other words, you want people to do all this research because the result is they spend more money.

When you look at the Google data you can see that the items that people can interact with both online and offline tended to be the ones that took the longest to research. Items that are more easily sold online, such as financial services, tended to be purchased quickly. This difference could be due to the amount of offline research that people are conducting. In the retail world this is referred to as 'showrooming'. People go online to do some research, then they visit a retail store to see the product in 'real life' before going back home to do some more online research, perhaps finding something else and then visiting another shop to check out the alternative product. All of this adds delay to the buying process.

Buyers rarely go online and buy something without checking out the alternatives. They do this in a variety of ways, sometimes checking other websites, sometimes going into shops or visiting potential suppliers. Gone are the days when people compared just a couple of potential products or suppliers, now they do a lot of 'homework'.

The reason for this is to do with the psychology of risk. Buying something involves risk – we risk making the wrong purchase, spending money unnecessarily, for instance. So, we seek to minimize that risk. But if there is more information around on any product or service we want to check out everything, in our bid to minimize the risks. Hence, the more information available via the web, the more research people will do in order to satisfy their inner need for risk reduction. As a result, people are making multiple checks and taking much longer to choose items than would have been the case in the past.

In practical terms this means that sales people need to be able to provide multiple 'touch points' for product and service information. Remember, the Google study found that shopping baskets were higher for people who had done more initial research. So, by having more research possibilities for your customers you will increase the value of your sales. Apart from having information available on websites, it means ensuring that it is tied in to offline information such as leaflets or in-store displays. With the rise in showrooming and its equivalent in services, you need to ensure that your online and offline worlds are fully integrated so that potential customers have a consistent experience.

Another potential way of ensuring that you offer people greater research possibilities is through the use of 'sequential autoresponders'. These are a series of emails that are automatically triggered every few days after people show an initial interest in your products. Each email can alert them to more information, giving them links to suitable additional material. The emails can also be a means of getting people to revisit your website. The Google study found that people often went back again and again to websites for information – hence triggering those return visits through regular emails you are enabling people to do what they want to do in terms of research. Also, remember that the Google study found that people tended to buy things up to 80 days after their initial research. Without a sequential autoresponder lasting for three months or so it would be easy to forget those potential customers who visited you so long ago. But with the automated responder emails going out, you would be more likely to capture those future sales.

The other important thing to consider is the amount of information you provide either online or in printed documents, for instance. The behaviour of shoppers is such that they are now seeking more and more in-depth and detailed information than ever before. That means web pages or brochures need to carry lots of detail and background material to help people get enough information to help them reduce their risk of purchase. Do that, and they will be more likely to buy from you. In addition, if you provide plenty of outlets for that information, you create more 'touch points' and, as Google explains, the value of those sales goes up. The changes in buyer behaviour at first sight seem to work against sales people, but by tapping into that behaviour for risk reduction you can actually increase your chances of selling at the same time as raising the value of those sales.

So what are the big takeaways here?

- **People conduct in-depth buying research:** People take a long time these days to research what they want to buy – and they do lots of in-depth research.
- **People want to buy instantly:** You need to be set up to cope with instant decision-making, allowing people to get immediately what they want.
- **People make rapid decisions to buy:** Once the research is completed by the consumer, the buying decision is made rapidly these days.

Source

'Beyond last click: Understanding your consumers' online path to purchase' (2011) (Google, Mountain View, California)

See also

Chapter 5 – Most sales journeys start online

Chapter 27 – Cold calls weaken sales

Chapter 34 – Forecasting the future depends on staff knowledge

Chapter 36 – Transparency in sales extends online

Further reading

Graves, Philip, *Consumer.ology: The Truth about Consumers and the Psychology of Shopping* (Nicholas Brealey Publishing, London, 2013)

www.nielsen.com/eu/en.html

Journal of Direct, Data and Digital Marketing Practice (2014) Vol. 15 pp 317–26

16 SELLING TO MEN OR WOMEN IS NOT THE SAME

*Female buyers want complete solutions
but male buyers are not so specific*

There are more women in the world than men; biology and natural selection combine to tip the balance of the genders towards females. Yet in spite of the world being this way, business has – until recently – been dominated by men. That is gradually changing with more women getting top jobs and more women taking an interest in business, thanks to schools and universities spending more time on teaching business studies. So, one thing is for sure: there are going to be more sales women in the future. The chances are they will quickly learn how to sell to men. There remains a question mark, however, over whether – despite all their years dominating sales – men have ever truly learned to sell to women.

In a review of studies on male and female management behaviour, the University of Connecticut found that in spite of suggestions to the contrary, there is very little in the way of differences between the sexes. The research review found that, largely, men and women are pretty much the same. However, even though men and women tend to behave the same for the most part, there are some subtle differences revealed by research that are important in the sales environment.

In a study of small and medium-sized enterprises researchers from the University of Connecticut and Northeastern University found that women benefit in the workplace from their family and the support they get from them. However, male entrepreneurs did not show any impact from such connections. What this study suggests is that it isn't necessarily the way women behave that is any different to men, but the way the world treats women leads to different responses.

This is highlighted in a study conducted at West Virginia University that looked at different types of sales approaches and the responses to such approaches from men and women buyers. The researchers investigated three kinds of selling – product selling, solution selling and provocation selling. Product selling is when a sales person merely has an item to sell and runs through its features and benefits. Solution selling is about asking questions, finding out the problems the customer has and then suggesting a specific solution using the products or services a sales person is trying to sell. Provocation-based selling is when the sales person identifies issues and problems within the business of which the buyer is not even aware.

The research looked at the way women and men responded to each of these different kinds of sales approach. The product-based sales approach was largely ineffective for both genders. Generally, people do not like it. Product-based selling increased conflict between the sales person and the buyer. You can see why: a sales person turns up – even for a booked appointment – and then proceeds to reel off a whole list of supposed benefits, hands over a brochure and asks how many do you want. It is uninspiring and perceived as a time-wasting exercise by the potential buyer. Yet, in spite of these obvious feelings, product-based selling is a significant activity, with thousands of businesses using it every day. One thing the West Virginia study found out about product-based selling was that it tended to annoy women even more than it annoyed men.

When it came to the provocation style of selling, no one liked it. Men and women were equal in their dislike of provocation-style selling. In spite of this, many firms try to sell in this way. The idea, apparently, is to make customers realize they have a problem that needs fixing and that the sales person has the perfect solution. But people do not like being told they have a problem; they prefer to identify that for themselves.

Perhaps this is why solution-based selling was the most 'likeable' of the three selling approaches used in the West Virginia research. Importantly, the researchers found that the solution-based approach led to the sales person being viewed as more trustworthy than any of the other sales methods on test. This impact was most strongly felt in women buyers – they liked solution-based selling more than men. Indeed, sometimes male buyers found that solution-based selling produced a small level of conflict.

This study shows us that women prefer solutions-based sales approaches over and above any other kind of selling method. However, it may not be some kind of in-built preference. As the review from the University of Connecticut found, there are few actual differences between the behaviour of male and female managers. The differences appear to be coming from the way women are treated. Perhaps sales people are trying to avoid conflict with women more than they do with men. This would lead to a solution-based approach that would be more acceptable, to men and women. But if the avoidance of conflict happens more with women buyers it is no wonder they like solutions-selling more than men. Another issue could be that more sales people are male and that a solutions-based selling situation with other men is more controlled by inter-male rivalry coming into play, thereby increasing conflict and making solutions-selling less attractive to male buyers.

It is clearly a complex set of behaviours that need further analysis, but what is clear is that women really do like solutions-based selling. So if your buyer is female, you ought to opt for that approach over and above any other technique you may want to use. In other words, you need to adapt your sales approach according to the situation you find yourself in, as discussed in Chapter 2.

It also means that you need to be certain to use a solutions-based approach if your buyer is female. That might mean you need to understand solutions-selling better and if you can then get a grasp of solutions-selling you will be able to sell better to women and avoid conflict with men, especially if you are male yourself.

In fact, solution-based selling is a bit like being a doctor. You start off nice and friendly, building rapport, allowing the buyer to relax. Then you ask questions to 'diagnose' the situation the buyer finds themselves in. Solutions-based selling, like medical diagnosis, is full of questions. Indeed, most of the time you will be asking questions, nodding, saying 'uh-huh' a lot and letting your customer unburden themselves. The more talking they do and the less speaking you do, so much the better.

Having listened to them talk about their situation you can then begin to offer solutions, much like a doctor might weigh up what they were told and then offer some potential treatments. You would then discuss those treatment options with the doctor and together you would decide the route ahead. The same is true for the solutions sales person. They offer a range of potential solutions to the issues uncovered in the 'diagnosis' session. Then together with the customer a route forward is mapped out, including the purchase of relevant products and services to 'ease the pain'.

It is interesting that doctors are generally a highly trusted profession. We actually assume they know what they are talking about. But when we are with a doctor a lot of the time all they are doing is asking us questions and listening to what we say. It is this factor that appears to be related to their trustworthiness. The West Virginia study found that trustworthiness was greatest when sales people used solutions-based selling. That is telling because it suggests that the sales people who spent most of their time listening were behaving somewhat like doctors who are trusted because of that kind of behaviour.

How, though, do you start the 'diagnosis' session without speaking very much? Doctors do this by reading your notes in advance and by observing things carefully – noticing the way you walk in and sit down, for instance. In other words they have done their homework in advance. Solutions-based selling needs to do the same. You need to have researched your customers and their competition before you even set foot in the building. Or if you sell in retail, for instance, you need to observe the customer before they even approach you. In other words, do your own homework. This will then give you a starting point for any discussion about the situation your customer finds themselves in.

Men and women might not behave as differently as we might think. But our response to them is often different. Sales people may need to adjust their own behaviour in order to gain more sales from women by being much more of a 'doctor' than a pushy sales person.

So what are the big takeaways here?

- **Solutions-selling works best for female customers:** Women prefer solution-based sales approaches more than any other kind of selling.
- **Knowing your customers increases solutions-selling potential:** Discover how to sell from a solutions perspective. To do this you will also need to research your customers more.
- **Avoid conflict when providing solutions:** Women do not like conflict in product-based selling. If you have products to sell, focus on the solutions they provide if you are selling to women.

Sources

Powell, G. N. (1990), 'One More Time: Do Female and Male Managers Differ?', *Academy of Management Perspectives*, Vol. 4 No. 3 pp 68–75

Powell, G. N. & Eddleston, K. A. (2013), 'Linking family-to-business enrichment and support to entrepreneurial success: Do female and male entrepreneurs experience different outcomes?' *Journal of Business Venturing*, Vol. 28 Issue 2 pp 261–80

Wood, J. A., Johnson, J., Boles, J. S. & Barksdale, H. (2014), 'Investigating sales approaches and gender in customer relationships', *Journal of Business & Industrial Marketing*, Vol. 29 Issue 1 pp 11–23

See also

Chapter 2 – Adaptive selling is vital

Chapter 17 – How to sell to silver surfers

Chapter 18 – Get inside the mind of your buyer

Chapter 26 – Mindfulness can cut conflict

Further reading

Eades, Keith M., *The New Solution Selling: The Revolutionary Sales Process That is Changing the Way People Sell* (McGraw-Hill, New York, 2003)

Gray, John, *Men Are from Mars, Women Are from Venus* (Harper Element, London, 2013)

Hoberman, Judy, *Selling In A Skirt: The Secrets Women Don't Know They Know about Sales* (Next Century Publishing, 2014)

HOW TO SELL TO SILVER SURFERS

*Each generation buys things slightly differently
than the previous generation*

Silver surfers are those people who use the Internet but who
have grey hair. That's a lot of people – especially as your hair
can start going grey in your 20s...! There is a plethora of
books, magazines and websites all dedicated to helping older
generations cope with modern technology, as though they were
all technically illiterate. Sometimes the people producing such
items seem to forget that the people who invented most of our
modern technology are in their 60s and 70s. Indeed, the man
who invented the very basis on which Internet communications
work, Vint Cerf, celebrated his 70th birthday in 2013. He most
definitely has silver hair (and beard) but it is doubtful he needs
technical advice. There is a widespread assumption that people
with grey hair can't use the Internet. Like many assumptions it
is largely false. After all, there are people blogging these days in
their 80s and 90s. Besides which, the first-ever online purchase
was made by a 72-year-old lady called Mrs Jane Snowball back
in 1984 in Gateshead before the World Wide Web was invented.
You can hardly say that older people do not use modern
technology.

It is the assumption, though, that they cannot, which leads many
businesses to believe they need to treat older people in some
special way, different to the rest of their younger customers.
That might or might not be true, so it is good that researchers
from California State University have reviewed the best ways to
sell to the generations. What they have discovered is that there
are indeed things you need to consider for each generation – not
just older people; younger people need certain types of sales
approaches too.

The Californian study was a review of several other studies reported in the academic literature. In assessing what studies had discovered, the researchers split the generations into six groups:

Pre Depression	Born before 1930
Depression	Born 1930–1945
Baby Boom	Born 1946–1964
Generation X	Born 1965–1976
Generation Y	Born 1977–1993
Generation Z	Born after 1994

The researchers considered studies that had shown how each generation responded to particular methods of selling and there are some quite interesting differences that were uncovered. For instance, the older generations tend to have plenty of money, though not all of it disposable as much of it is tied up in property and possessions. Even so, people who may not be generally targeted by sales people appear to have the available cash to buy things. Furthermore, contrary to expectations, the Depression age group tends to be quite active; they are not all stuck at home doing nothing. The research suggests, therefore, that if sales people view this older generation as being at home with little money to spend and so not worth contacting, they need to think again.

What the Californian research showed was the need to treat these older buyers with considerable respect. They come from a more formal era and so they much prefer being called by their title and last name. They also expect more communication in printed form – but that does not mean they cannot or will not use the Internet. However, if you are targeting these seniors using modern technology you need to take into account their inevitably failing eyesight. Larger type sizes in emails help, for example.

When it comes to the Baby Boomer generation, the researchers found that this group of people are generally quite self-centred. They like quick fixes and they do not like authority. Hence they like sales people to get to the point and to provide solutions that will work almost immediately. However, one characteristic of the Baby Boomer is that they are frequently changing their buying behaviour. They have been brought up through eras of change and so they adapt and change themselves too. Even so, they prefer simplicity in terms of communication, say the researchers. No fancy complex messaging is needed – get straight to the point.

The Generation X individual, though, tends to be more educated than earlier generations and so they are very questioning. That means they prefer transparency, say the researchers. The Generation X individual doesn't like sales patter or advertising – they see straight through it. Generation X individuals want your sales approach to be direct but they will frequently refer your ideas to their peers because they value social recommendation and support.

In terms of the Generation Y people, these tend to be image driven and want people to recognize them for their uniqueness. The researchers found that this generation expects things to be customizable to their individual needs. Plus Generation Y individuals tend to be group-focused with plenty of sharing. This generation has grown up with the Internet and so they expect sales people to use technology efficiently.

The final Generation Z group has never lived in a world without the Internet and so the web and other technologies are crucial to this generation. The researchers also found that this generation is driven by group and family values. Peer acceptance is fundamental to this group of consumers. Generation Z has also grown up in a time when financial services have become available to young age groups, meaning that many of them are able to buy things independently of parents or grandparents, using their own money. Having said that, the Californian researchers point out that this generation also has products and services bought for them by older generations or parents and grandparents.

Gaining an understanding of the key elements of each generation should help sales people find better ways of getting their messages across. To do that, however, you need to know or estimate the age of your customer so you can choose the appropriate communication method. It is also important not to make assumptions. It is easy to assume that older people do not use the Internet, when this is not true. Equally, it is easy to think that the youngest generation is only motivated by personal excitement, when the research shows they have strong family values.

The Californian research showed that the younger generations are more group-orientated, something which is borne out by a study conducted at Kingston Business School in the UK. This found that older shoppers tend to be more conservative, sticking to their regular brands, for example. However, the research found that this was partly due to the smaller social groups of the older shoppers. This exposed them to much fewer word-of-mouth recommendations than younger generations.

Taken together these two studies would suggest that sales people do need to consider their communication methods for older generations compared with their younger customers. Older people do use technology but are prone to not having enough social activity to benefit from word of mouth. That means it might make sense for sales people to consider using social networking programs to reach their older targets. Counterintuitive this may be, but it could well be the way to generate more electronic word of mouth among a target group that has money to spend.

So what are the big takeaways here?

- **Sales techniques depend on age of customer:** Older generations need different sales techniques to those born in the Internet age.
- **Be sure you know the age ranges of your customers:** Make sure you know the age of your customers, or at least which generation they fit into.
- **Older generations get less information in advance:** Older people tend to receive less information about potential purchases, making their decision-making less effective.

Sources

East, R., Uncles, M. D. & Lomax, W. (2013), 'Hear nothing, do nothing: The role of word of mouth in the decision-making of older consumers', *Journal of Marketing Management*, Vol. 30 Issue 7–8 pp 786–801

Williams K. C. and Page R. A. (2011), 'Marketing to the Generations', *Journal of Behavioural Studies in Business*, Vol. 3 April

See also

Chapter 15 – Buyers behave differently now

Chapter 16 – Selling to men or women is not the same

Chapter 22 – Upselling works through customer focus

Further reading

Codrington, Graeme and Grant-Marshall, Sue, *Mind the Gap* (Portfolio Penguin, London, 2011)

Fromm, Jeff and Garton, Christie, *Marketing to Millennials: Reach the Largest and Most Influential Generation of Consumers Ever* (AMACOM, New York, 2013)

https://www.youtube.com/watch?v=_Qvn0pAcxcg

18 GET INSIDE THE MIND OF YOUR BUYER

Sales people who get the most sales understand their buyers as people

Some men seem to experience the pain of childbirth. Indeed, there is a hotly debated condition known as the Couvade Syndrome where men experience pregnancy symptoms along with their partner. For years, doctors have thought this is a psychosomatic condition, but research shows that the men may indeed have hormonal changes that mimic what their partner is going through. It is not as strange as it may seem. Women who work together often find that their menstrual cycles begin to alter slightly, with those who work closely together discovering that their cycles have synchronized. It would seem that we can alter our internal workings just by being in the presence of another person.

Part of the possible reason for this kind of phenomenon was discovered in 1999 at the University of Parma in Italy by neuroscientist, Giacomo Rizzolatti. He was monitoring the brain activity in a group of monkeys in the laboratory. He noticed that there were sudden spikes of activity in brain regions associated with food when the lab assistants were handling food. Further investigation showed that the motor neurons – the brain cells that control movement – were also firing up, as though the monkey itself were handling the food. This was the discovery of what are known as 'mirror neurons'. These are brain cells that become active when we observe other people doing something. For instance, when someone touches something hot and moves their hand away, your mirror neurons will mimic the action as though you yourself had been burned. You will even sense the shock and the potential pain.

Since those initial findings with monkeys, Dr Rizzolatti has investigated the whole area of mirror neurons and has made some startling discoveries. For instance, mirror neurons appear to be responsible for the reception of emotions. Imagine you are at a circus and the high wire act is making everyone 'ooh' and 'aah'. How do you think that the entire audience manages to do that in unison? After all, the wobbling of the acrobat on the tightrope needs to be assessed by our brains and then we need to work out what emotional response we have to it. Some people would clearly be able to do that more quickly than others because they may have greater cognitive skills. Yet, as you know, when the high wire artist wobbles, the 'oohs' and the 'aahs' all happen in unison. This is because of mirror neurons. When you are watching the tightrope walker your brain's mirror neurons are replicating the balancing act. And as soon as there is a wobble, your mirror neurons reproduce that wobble and so you experience the sense of danger, enabling everyone to 'ooh' and 'aah' at the same moment. There is no need for your brains to work anything out because the mirror neurons allow you to experience the wobble at the same time. Because everyone in the audience is having the same experience, there is no delay as nothing needs thinking about. Everyone has experienced the wobble at the same time as the acrobat.

An important discovery in the research about mirror neurons was that these special brain cells can also be triggered even if we cannot see the action, but imagine it. The researchers showed the monkeys some food and then placed a barrier in front of the item to hide it. Then the researcher reached behind the barrier to pick up the food, without showing it. The mirror neurons of the monkeys fired into action, showing that these special brain cells become active without us having to observe something. That could partly explain why we get emotionally involved with a movie or TV programme – our mirror neurons fire up because we are using our imagination and then sensing something.

For instance, horror movies often do not show the 'monster'. It is up to our imaginations to work out what it might be like; we experience the fear without actually observing anything. The way this works is demonstrated in the movie *North by Northwest*, where the director, Alfred Hitchcock makes the audience think one thing, while actually delivering another. The hero, played by Cary Grant, is reaching over the side of something – the viewer is not sure what – and is trying to pull a woman upwards, the viewer assumes to safety. When you watch it, your mirror neurons will be firing and you will be sensing the danger thanks to your imagination. Just like the monkeys who were mentally grasping something they could not see, the master of suspense movies makes your brain sense the danger. Except there is no danger – the camera pulls outwards where we discover that Cary Grant's character is attempting to lift up his new wife into the top bunk of the sleeper train they are in. The viewer's mirror neurons make them sense something that is different to reality – a factor exploited by many thriller movies and by comedians too.

What this means in terms of sales is significant. It means that what you touch, show, do or feel is being sensed by the person you are speaking with. This has huge implications for sales. If, for instance, you do not 'buy in' to the product you are selling, you will 'give the game away' with your body language. That will be impacting on the mirror neurons of your customer, who will sense some tension. This will happen at a subconscious level – they will not necessarily be aware of what is happening or that you do not fully support the product you are trying to sell to them. But they will feel something is not quite right because their mirror neurons will be replicating your own hesitancy with the item.

In a similar way, if you do not fully understand what you are trying to sell, a customer will subconsciously be able to sense this because of activity in their mirror neurons associated with your hesitant behaviour when answering questions, for example.

If you want to be sure of a sale, the mere presence of mirror neuron activity in your customers means that you have to fully demonstrate your passion and knowledge for everything you sell. Sometimes a sales person sees a customer and does not make the sale. They come away from the encounter saying 'they didn't want to buy anyway'. But perhaps this attitude was present in advance of the sales appointment and so the mirror neurons were actively picking up those negative signals and suggesting subconsciously 'do not buy'. Not only do you need to convey full knowledge about your products and services, but preconceived views of the customer can also influence a sales person's behaviour, which is then picked up by the mirror neurons of the customer, thereby influencing them to buy or not to buy.

There are, though, some positive impacts of mirror neurons. Customers are not the only people who have them; sales people have mirror neurons too. So that means your mirror neurons will be activated when you watch the customer. You will feel how they feel when you observe them closely. Imagine being back in that circus tent again with the tightrope walker – you only 'ooh' and 'aah' at the right time when you are watching the acrobat. If you look down at your programme, or see where the candy floss seller has got to, you miss the action up in the roof and your mirror neurons stop working. It means that you cannot benefit from your own mirror neurons letting you know what customers are feeling unless you watch them, like a hawk. A good sales person is a detailed observer of customers. The more you observe, the more your mirror neurons will fire up and the more you will start to experience and feel what they are feeling. Once you know that, you can make more sales because you will begin to understand where they are coming from.

The Italian research suggests there is a lot more to discover about mirror neurons. Other neuroscientists disagree with some of the findings and suggestions. But what is not disputed is their existence. It means that there is a hidden level of communication between a sales person and their customer. They know more about you than you think and you know more about them than they think. You are going to increase the likelihood of sales when you use this two-way communication to let customers know you really love your products or services and when you observe them you can detect how they feel.

So what are the big takeaways here?

- **Buyers are influenced by the sales person's behaviour:** Buyers' brains are influenced directly by what sales people do, say and feel.

- **You need to be sure you demonstrate true knowledge of your products:** Make sure you truly understand in depth everything you sell.
- **You must like what you sell:** If you do not truly feel good about what you sell, buyers will be able to tell without consciously knowing what the problem is; they will have a negative frame of mind if you behave negatively.

Source

Rizzolatti, G., Fogassi, L. & Gallese, V. (2006), 'Mirrors In The Mind', *Scientific American*, Vol. 295 pp 54–61

See also

Chapter 14 – Avoid too much eye contact with customers

Chapter 19 – Spotting those buying signals

Chapter 23 – Posing powerfully boosts negotiations

Further reading

Hazeldine, Simon, *Neuro-Sell: How Neuroscience Can Power Your Sales Success* (Kogan Page, London, 2014)

Keysers, Christian, *The Empathic Brain* (Social Brain Press, Amsterdam, 2011)

www.neurosciencemarketing.com/blog/articles/mirror-neurons.htm

www.kevinhogan.com/mirror-neurons-intro.htm

19 SPOTTING THOSE BUYING SIGNALS

Body language gives away whether customers are in the buying mood

Customers are never in a neutral kind of mood. They are always excited, doubtful, worried or in some other emotional state. They might be buying something for themselves that they have long desired, putting them in a good mood. Or they may be at the end of a long day, desperately looking for a present for their great aunt and have been uninspired by everything they have seen, making them tired and frustrated. Equally, in a B2B scenario a buyer can be in a depressed state because they have spent all day meeting a range of potential suppliers and seeing you is just one more presentation they have to listen to. They are bored. Whether you work in retail or in professional services, your customers always carry a mood of some kind.

Psychologists refer to mood as 'affect'. It is a kind of spectrum where you might have hugely 'positive affect', a glowing positive feeling you get when you have won the marathon or just had sex. It is a 'high'. Then you can get a completely 'negative affect', where you are the lowest of your lows, totally lifeless, such as when someone close to you dies. Between these two extremes of the highs and lows, we have a variety of moods on this spectrum of 'affect'.

Researchers at the Saïd Business School at Oxford University conducted an interesting series of experiments in 2013 to see if there was any relationship between a sales person being able to spot the level of 'affect' of a customer and how that individual rated the buying experience. In other words, they wanted to find out whether spotting the mood of the customer had any kind of connection to how that customer perceived the sales person and the sales process. In particular, the researchers were interested in discovering whether there was any link between a salesperson detecting the 'affect' of customers without directly asking their mood, but just using body language and facial expressions.

In one experiment the customer was supposedly buying a jumper for their roommate – the participants observing and rating the behaviour were university students. However, in one scenario the customer indicated they were not really that much interested in buying the jumper. They did this by talking to the sales person while standing next to a display of jeans, touching them and looking at them all the time they were talking about buying a jumper for their friend. This was designed to suggest to the salesperson that the customer was not really in the mood for buying something for somebody else – what they really wanted was to buy jeans for themselves.

The research assistants playing the role of the customer had been given extensive training to display certain type of facial expressions or body language to demonstrate one of two moods – either being interested in the jumper for their friend, or actually preferring to get jeans for themselves. Those playing the part of the sales person responded either well or badly to either facial expressions or body language. This led to four possibilities – good response to facial expressions, poor response to them, good response to body language and a bad response to it.

The participants in the study then had to rate how well the sales person responded to the relevant body language signals or facial expressions. It was quite complicated analysis, but the final results showed that when the sales person was able to read the relevant cues about the mood – either through facial expressions or body language – then they were perceived as giving a good sales experience.

In a second experiment, the Oxford researchers wanted to see if the view of the sales person's ability was different if an individual was a customer or an observer. They wanted to see if you had to actually be involved in the sales situation to rate the process as good as a result of the sales person accurately detecting mood. Would an observer rate the sales experience as good if they had just seen a sales person do their job well, or do we have to be directly involved?

This experiment showed we have to be involved. Merely observing a good sales person accurately deal with the body language signals of another customer is not enough for us to think the sales person is providing a great experience. As observers we seem to expect that the good behaviour of a sales person is what should happen. But once we are involved directly in the encounter we change our view and we 'up-rate' our view, suggesting the sales experience is more positive.

These experiments in this Oxford study have important implications for sales people. Together they suggest that being able to accurately read and respond well to body language signals and facial expressions of mood means that customers will rate their sales experience more highly. Having the right product knowledge is expected – but having empathy with the customer and responding to their mood appears to be significant in customers having a positive view of their sales experience.

What this means in practical terms is that sales managers may need to consider the kind of people they employ as sales people. Consideration should be given to ensuring that people with high levels of empathy and what you might call 'emotional intelligence' are likely to be good at providing customers with a positive experience, thanks to their ability to detect 'affect' or the mood of the customer.

Equally, the Oxford research suggests that firms should think about the kind of training they provide to sales people. It may well be that sales managers and team leaders need to ensure that training courses help people understand body language as it applies to determining mood.

Another practical consideration, discussed by the Oxford researchers, is the need to consider the layout and design of sales environments. Are they conducive to helping assess or improve 'affect'? Equally, are your working practices set up to allow sales staff to spend sufficient time with customers to be able to detect mood non-verbally and to adjust the sales situation to suit? If the sales environment and the working practices mean that customers feel rushed through in a non-private or personal space, you are less likely to have them report positive experiences. Making customers feel they are getting personal attention in a personal space is one thing, but you also need to have skilled staff who can detect and understand the mood of the customers, because by doing that you will get them to feel more positive about your company's products and services.

The researchers also point out that people can practise body language skills. Having regular practice and feedback sessions could be part of the everyday sales culture within your business so that everyone on the team can improve their abilities in determining mood.

What this all really points to is the need to empathize with your customers and to see everything from their perspective, Part of that perspective is going to be the mood they are in. Take into account that mood by properly analysing body language and facial expressions and your sales operation will benefit.

So what are the big takeaways here?

- **Be sure to check customer body language:** Reading the mood of a customer correctly using body language signals makes them rate their sales experience more highly.
- **Be aware of the mood of a customer:** Concentrate on body language signals that show the mood someone is in so you can empathize.
- **Show the customer you care about them as an individual:** Customers like it when you pay detailed attention to their body language and facial expressions.

Source

Puccinelli, N. M. et al (2013), 'The value of knowing what customers really want: The impact of salesperson ability to read non-verbal cues of affect on service quality', *Journal of Marketing Management* Vol. 29 Nos. 3–4, pp 356–73

See also

Chapter 2 – Adaptive selling is vital

Chapter 14 – Avoid too much eye contact with customers

Chapter 18 – Get inside the mind of your buyer

Chapter 23 – Posing powerfully boosts negotiations

Further reading

Arden, Derek, *The Secret Language of Success* (Tiptree House Publishing, Guildford, 2003)

Collett, Peter, *The Book of Tells* (Bantam, London, 2004)

www.forbes.com/sites/nickmorgan/2012/10/25/7-surprising-truths-about-body-language

20 CLOSING SALES IS NOT NECESSARY

Forget 'close techniques' — they simply do not work

You don't get a sale until the person has signed on the dotted line or handed over the money. That's a given, of course. But getting people to part with their cash is often seen as the ultimate sales skill. In the jargon of sales, of course, it is known as 'the close'. Unless you 'close the sale', so the theory goes, no sale has been made.

So popular is the notion of the 'sales close' that there are entire training courses devoted to it. One listing of closing techniques has 72 of them, from the 'Golden Bridge Close' to the 'Thermometer Close'. In the Golden Bridge Close, apparently, you make all the other options seem less attractive and desirable, which means your offer becomes instantly much more attractive. In the Thermometer Close you ask a series of questions on a scale of 1 to 10. You take the customer down a road of questioning so that they inevitably score high numbers, allowing you then to leap in and sell or get them to the next stage of the selling process. Because they have scored what you want them to do so highly, they can't back out. You just keep turning up the heat on them.

Sales people of the 'old school' would keep their favourite closing techniques with them at all times like a little toolkit they would bring out to deal with any situation where they thought the customer might be backing away.

The trouble with any closing the sale technique is that customers can see them coming. As soon as a sales person starts using any of the closing techniques they have been taught, the customer starts to back off anyway, naturally – making it even harder for the sale to take place.

The whole issue of closing techniques has been exposed in several pieces of academic research, but one study into sales person 'types' reveals some interesting findings. This research was carried out at Cranfield School of Management and the University of Bath. The researchers investigated the behaviours of 800 different sales people and were able to classify them into eight different types. Each of the types discovered was dominated by particular behaviour patterns.

The 'Focusers' were people who were so interested in what they were selling they went into every last detail about what was on offer, regardless of whether or not the customer needed to know this information. Almost one in five sales people in the research was identified as a 'Focuser'.

The 'Narrators' were people who stuck to the script. They were people who used the company's training and marketing materials to say exactly what they had been told and no more. Once asked questions, they struggled. Narrators made up 15 per cent of the 800 sales people.

'Socializers' made up another 15 per cent of the research group. These were sales people who are very friendly and form a good personal relationship with the customer. But that's about all they do. To them, a sales call is a chance to have a chat and a catch-up.

The 'Consultants' comprised another 15 per cent slice of the 800 sales people. These people listen, seek to solve problems and are the people who focus on solutions-based selling. But they get so focused on providing the solution to a single problem, they often fail to see beyond it.

The next most common category of sales people were the 'Closers', representing 13 per cent of the 800 participants in the study. These individuals were mostly selling products and were keen to use all those 'closing' techniques they had been taught. These were people who simply had to get the sale.

The 'Experts' represented 9 per cent of the group. They kept their customers happy and seemed to sell without trying. Experts were the top sales achievers out of the 800 participants in the study yet seemed to sell without any real effort.

'Storytellers' were sales people who just loved to give examples and case histories. They chatted a lot about how other people were using their products and services. Their meetings were long and often they did not sell anything. Yet 7 per cent of the group were 'Storytellers'.

Finally, the eighth category of sales people comprised the 'Aggressors'. These people just simply wanted to get the sale. They did not want to negotiate; they just wanted to get the sale done. They appeared to be in competition with the customer. Some 7 per cent of the group were 'Aggressors'.

Overall, the study found that out of 800 sales people only 37 per cent of them (296) were consistently good at selling. Indeed, one in every 250 of them exceeded their sales targets. Of all the sales meetings in which this group of 800 people took part, only 9.1 per cent of them resulted in a sale.

This study does not provide very good support for the sales profession. Largely, it suggests that much of what they do is worthless and negative. The study found some clues as to why this is. It identified four sets of behaviour that were linked to successful sales – good advanced preparation, interacting with the customer, the quality of the presentation and how the sales person dealt with challenges. Unrelated to success was the pitch itself, the rapport built through the presentation and storytelling (use of case studies).

The groups who were trying to close sales tended to focus on the activities unrelated to sales success. Indeed the 'Closers' group of sales people tended to do much more of these negative behaviours and very few of the successful ones. The 'Experts' did a considerable amount of the positive behaviour, which seemed to counter the impact of the negatives that they also did. Perhaps they did these because a lot of sales training focuses on gaining rapport, doing the presentation, using case studies and closing the sale. Yet this research suggests that those are precisely the kind of behaviours that make it more difficult to get someone to buy. Indeed, the study shows that all of the sales people, including the 'Experts' do a lot of those negative things. Is it any wonder that most sales calls do not end in a purchase?

What this study suggests is that behaviour needs to shift away from focusing on 'the sale' and move towards better preparation and then lots of interaction with the customer based on that solid research. These days there is no excuse for not doing considerable amounts of advanced research. You can use the company's website to find out a great deal about them. You can track their activities on social media. You can see what their customers are saying about them on social networks too. Not only that, you can find out about their competitive situation, read articles about them in online trade periodicals and check out their news on Google News or News360. If you want, you can even ask questions about them on Twitter or LinkedIn, for example. There is no reason these days why a sales person cannot do intense preparation in advance of each sales meeting.

If you consider that 91.9 per cent of all sales meetings are failures because they do not achieve a sale, the good sales person could cut down the number of sales meetings they go to and use that time instead to prepare well for the meetings they are holding. This has implications for sales managers though. They often have the mindset that each sales person needs as many appointments as possible. The theory is, the more appointments they have, the more sales they will make. It is a numbers game. There is some truth in that – the more people you see, the more you will sell. But this research shows that it is about preparation and knowing the customer so well you can interact effectively. That implies that sales managers need to focus less on numbers of appointments and more on preparation and results achieved. Often, sales managers provide monthly targets to sales people listing the number of meetings they should attend. Sales people work flat out to attend all those appointments to reach their target. It is chasing appointments for appointments' sake.

The whole sales arena is focused on getting lots of appointments and 'closing the sale' in as many as possible. That appears to lead to a 9.1 per cent success rate. The research shows, however, that the success rate goes up when you focus less on closing the sale and more on knowing and deeply understanding your customer. That suggests sales managers also need to re-look at the way they target their sales team.

So what are the big takeaways here?

- **Forget the whole notion of closing sales:** Closing the sale is old-fashioned and out-dated and doesn't work well with modern, well-informed buyers.
- **Allow customers to decide to buy:** Seek to build supportive relationships so that customers make the inevitable decision to buy from you.
- **The more planning you do, the better:** The best sales people are those who do considerable amounts of advanced planning and preparation before meeting a customer.

Sources

Bonney, F. Leff & Williams, Brian C. (2009),'From products to solutions: the role of salesperson opportunity recognition', *European Journal of Marketing*, Vol. 43 Issue 7/8 pp 1032–52

Ryals, L. J. & Davies, I. A. (2010), 'Do You Really Know Who Your Best Sales People Are?', *Harvard Business Review*, Vol. 88 No. 12

See also

Chapter 11 – Persistence pays in sales

Chapter 22 – Upselling works through customer focus

Chapter 25 – Kindness kills objections

Further reading

Tovey, David, *Principled Selling: How to win more business without selling your soul* (Kogan Page, London, 2012)

Tracy, Brian, *The Art of Closing the Sale* (Thomas Nelson Publishing, Nashville, 2012)

trustedadvisor.com/articles/stop-trying-to-close-the-sale

changingminds.org/disciplines/sales/closing/closing_techniques.htm

21 CROSS-SELLING WORKS WHEN ALLOWED

Additional sales are most likely when sales staff know the entire product range

Most companies sell more than one kind of product or service. That means they often have dedicated sales teams or individuals who focus on a specific 'line'. These individuals then target companies most likely to buy those kind of products. However, most customers also buy a range of different products and services, using a variety of suppliers. A sales person who is at an appointment with a client may discover that the customer has another supplier providing them with the kind of products that they could also be supplying. Yet, because the sales person is not the relevant individual to sell those items – because they are part of another sales team's portfolio – the opportunity often gets lost.

Even without this situation arising, the chances of selling additional items to customers often gets missed because the client perceives the supplier as only selling a particular kind of product or service. For example, an office cleaning company may provide a range of additional property services such as buildings maintenance, but because the customer only thinks of them as a cleaning company they do not consider them for supplying maintenance. Instead, they look for an alternative supplier.

Many businesses lose out on the opportunity to 'cross-sell' – to provide customers with additional products and services that are beyond the scope of the individual sales person or outside the expectations of the customer. The 'pigeonholing' of both sales staff into product lines and suppliers into 'types' means that there are plenty of companies who do not sell as much as they could to their clients. This is wholly different to 'up-selling'

(See Chapter 22), which is the selling of additional products and services to enhance the original sale.

Research into the whole area of cross-selling has been conducted at Ruhr University Bochum in Germany and it found that three-quarters of all attempts to cross-sell ended in failure. The study wanted to find out if the difficulties with cross-selling were related to the sales force itself, or to other factors. It discovered that many of the issues were related to sales people and their management.

The researchers looked at 271 sales people working for a biotechnology company. These sales people represented 15 different 'divisions', which were grouped around sets of products and associated services. Sales people were selling from across all these product and service divisions into companies that had long-term buying processes, often two years or more. The study asked sales people about their perceived ability to cross-sell from across the range, as well as matching this to data from the company's sales records. In addition to this, 57 sales managers also completed questionnaires. In this way the German researchers hoped to be able to find out three things:

1. How the individual sales people perceived and attempted cross-selling
2. The actual results of those attempts to cross-sell
3. How the sales teams were managed and whether there was any link to that and cross-selling.

In addition, the researchers were able to see from the data they collected how well engaged with the entire product portfolio each sales person was. There were 15 different product divisions and so it was possible that each sales person could pick and choose.

The results showed that the more a sales person used the entire portfolio of products, the more cross-selling opportunities they took up. This suggests that knowing more about the entire range of products or services a company provides is a good way of being able to sell more because of that greater product or service knowledge. Importantly, though, the study found that the wider use of the company's entire portfolio of products was related to the behaviour of the sales leaders. When the sales managers were using 'transformational' techniques, the sales people were much more likely to use the entire range of company products and also did more cross-selling. Transformational leaders are people who focus on the morale and motivation of their staff. They are unlike 'transactional leaders', who concentrate on numbers, targets and so on.

The German study also provided some analysis as to the 'depth' of leadership. It found that there was a combination of Level 1 sales managers, who were managing sales leaders at Level 2 who were then running a sales team of their own. When the Level 1 and Level 2 sales leaders were both transformational and the sales people used a wide portfolio of products and services, the amount of cross-selling was at its highest. In other words, an environment of supportive, morale-raising people enables increased cross-selling to take place. This is in stark contrast to the teams that were transactionally led, and where cross-selling was weak.

What this all amounts to is the fact that opportunities for cross-selling are disappearing in companies where the sales culture is all about numbers and how much cash is generated. In the sales teams that had much less emphasis on this, cross-selling opportunities and performance were at their highest. In other words, when you allow your sales staff to stop focusing on targets, you actually make it easier for them to cross-sell and thereby increase their sales revenues.

This is another piece of research showing that the way sales teams are managed is linked to their performance. That, of course, is an obvious statement to any sales manager. But, like the research discussed in Chapter 20, it is another study which suggests that the constant focus on numbers and targets – which is the norm in many sales environments – is precisely the wrong thing to do if you want to increase sales. Companies are losing opportunities to cross-sell because they are focused on transactions.

The German research implies that the best way to ensure your company can take up as many cross-selling opportunities as possible is to have supportive and inspiring sales leaders who motivate staff to succeed, boosting their morale. However, that may require a change in company culture as well as a need for board directors, for instance, to focus less on the numbers and more on the results. The research shows that when sales people work in such environments they gain more widespread product knowledge and are able to cross-sell more as a result.

In practical terms, for many businesses the implications of this study in Germany may be hard to accept. For this reason it might be more appropriate to test out this theory. For instance, you could try the techniques on one particular sales team. You could remove from them the transactional focus and use a sales leader who is focused on motivation and morale boosting. Then you could compare their results in cross-selling to another sales team that is focused on transactions. That would demonstrate whether these techniques worked within your business and if the experiment proved positive you could then expand it to other teams.

If, however, you are an individual sales person, how can you increase your chances of being able to cross-sell? The research is clear – the wider your product knowledge, the more you are able to see those opportunities for cross-selling. That suggests you need to brush up your knowledge on all the products and services your company provides – even if you are not directly responsible for selling them. Start with your firm's own website and see what's on offer from those divisions of your business to which you have little exposure. In this way you will be able to know more about these areas and then you will be alert to opportunities should they arise while you are in discussion with customers. The research showed that the sales people using the widest portfolio of products and services were the ones with the highest amount of cross-selling. Essentially, the more you know about your company's products and services, the more you can sell.

Cross-selling opportunities clearly exist, but as the German study shows, companies are often not taking them up. A combination of management styles and restricted product or service knowledge combines to allow cross-selling opportunities to pass you by. If you want to be able to increase your sales as a result of selling additional and unrelated offerings to your clients, it is attitude that is the thing that needs changing. The attitude that sales are all about numbers is the key one to deal with. This study suggests that morale and motivation are more important.

So what are the big takeaways here?

- **Cross-selling depends on sales person behaviour:** The behaviour and knowledge of the sales person and their manager is crucial to the likelihood of a cross-sell being successful.
- **Know your products and services in depth:** Get as much knowledge about your company's products and services as possible – including those you are not responsible for selling.
- **Transactional sales reduce potential for cross-selling:** Cross-selling is much less likely to succeed when sales managers are focused on transactions.

Source

Schmitz, C., Lee, Y-C, and Lilien, G. L. (2014), Cross-Selling Performance in Complex Selling Contexts: An Examination of Supervisory- and Compensation-Based Controls, *Journal of Marketing*, Vol. 78 Issue 3 pp 1–19

See also

Chapter 22 – Upselling works through customer focus

Chapter 24 – Competitive selling needs low prices

Chapter 29 – Customers have no idea about prices

Chapter 40 – Sales staff must keep up to date with procedures

Further reading

Harding, Ford, *Cross-selling Success* (Adams Media Corporation, Avon, 2002)

www.forbes.com/sites/halahtouryalai/2012/01/25/the-art-of-the-cross-sell

www.smarta.com/advice/sales-and-marketing/sales/cross-selling-10-ways-to-sell-more-to-your-customer

22 UPSELLING WORKS THROUGH CUSTOMER FOCUS

Understanding the customer's precise needs makes additional sales more likely

Amazon has to be the world leader in upselling. Every time you add something to your virtual shopping basket the store's little elves have been busy preparing a selection of additional items that you might like to consider adding to your purchase. Order a laptop and the automated software will suggest you get a case to go with it. Choose a book and it will suggest a complementary title. Select even a loaf of bread and Amazon will suggest you might like to add some food bags to go with it to store your sandwiches in. You can't knock Amazon for trying.

What they are doing is no more than the oft-quoted classic line from McDonald's: 'Would you like fries with that?'. Go into any coffee shop nowadays and they're doing the same thing, suggesting you might like a pastry to go with your latte. Indeed, go into several high street retailers and as you are paying for your magazines, you are asked if you would like a huge slab of chocolate for a mere £1. It is all 'upselling' – getting you to buy something extra to increase the total value of the order.

Amazon, though, takes the world of upselling a stage further. In addition to suggesting extra items, it also suggests more expensive similar items to the one you are intending to buy. As you are viewing your selection the bottom of the screen shows you what other people bought after they had viewed the item you are considering. Many of those items are more expensive. Amazon is hoping you will desire these more expensive items because of the 'social proof' of other customers buying them.

You might have intended to buy the £300 laptop, but the social upsell has made you fork out £400.

This might all seem rather clever online – but is it worth it? Equally, is it really worth having slabs of chocolate for £1 for the few people who say 'yes please'? Essentially, is upselling really worthwhile? After all, you could spend a great deal of time and effort organizing and instigating upsells for relatively low returns. Furthermore, you run the risk of upsetting customers by repeatedly making offers they are not interested in.

Online, of course, it is easy to collect data and information on the benefits of upselling. We can be pretty sure it works for Amazon. They have been doing it for more than a decade. In 2012, Duracell tried an upsell campaign, called 'Do you want Duracell with that?' This was triggered when people bought a toy or some other item on Amazon that needed a battery. Compared with the same sales period in the previous year Duracell doubled its total amount of battery sales and increased its return on investment by 70 per cent. Furthermore, studies by SmartFocus show that online upsells are 20 times more effective than online cross-sells. Clearly upselling works, at least in the automated world of online sales.

Does it work in face-to-face selling though? That was the focus of research published by Yale University at the beginning of 2014. This study looked at the data from 150,000 sales transactions in the car rental sector at 100 different airports. The researchers classified the transactions into groups – those that were customer-facing and those that were not. Customer-facing transactions involved sales staff who spent much of their time face to face with customers. The non-customer-facing transactions were those that involved staff who do not normally deal with clients. Having divided the research data into these two main groups, each one was further subdivided into 'customer centric' or 'non-customer centric', focusing on levels of customer satisfaction. These two categories were based on the degree to which the transaction was focused on customer needs.

In addition to these measures, the researchers also looked at the management of the staff who made the sales and the associated upsells. The study wanted to identify if there was a relationship between the sales, the customer satisfaction and the way the sales person was managed. Typically in these car rental locations the sales staff were encouraged to upsell customers to a higher-priced model. There were five levels of models to which customers could be upgraded. The researchers took care to eliminate other factors that could make upselling easier, such as the level of technology provided to the sales teams in different locations.

In the final analysis the Yale study found that the customer-facing sales staff who were the most engaged and who focused their activity on customer-centric factors were the ones who were most able to upsell. What this really means is that the car rental staff who enjoy their jobs and who focus on the customer were the ones who upsold the most. A particular factor that connects all this together is customer satisfaction. That implies that satisfied customers are more amenable to upsells and a satisfied customer makes the sales person feel good too. It is a sort of feedback loop – happy customers make for happy staff that makes customers so happy they will buy the upgrade.

There is a further piece of research, though, linking sales performance – in this case upselling – to employee engagement that is not focused on targets. The researchers discuss the need for employees to be given a sense of accomplishment. Chasing numerical targets, once again, appears to work against the likelihood of improvements in sales.

What this means for sales managers is that in order to increase the chances of being able to gain upsells there needs to be a focus on motivating sales staff and building morale so they enjoy their jobs more. Happy staff makes for more upsells, it seems. Crucial to this, however, appears to be motivating them to improve customer satisfaction. That suggests that the sense of accomplishment sales staff feel could be linked to targets on customer satisfaction levels. Because the research showed that it is engaged staff who upsell more and that it is satisfied customers who buy more, then it makes sense to use customer satisfaction as your measure of staff involved in sales, rather than raw sales figures.

Another factor in the increased effectiveness of upselling revealed in the research is that length of tenure is a factor. Sales staff who have been around the business longer are effective at upselling. Clearly this is partly due to their greater depth of knowledge and experience. However, the fact that they have been in the business for a long period of time suggests significant engagement with their job. Finding out what makes people stay in your firm for longer periods of time can help you understand what factors are important in the way they are managed. Once you have that information you can use it to ensure more people stick around for longer periods of time. That in itself will inevitably lead to more upselling.

The other important factor to emerge from this Yale study is that people who are not customer-facing are much less able to make the upsell. That's because they clearly have less understanding of customer needs and are probably less experienced at sales. This means that sales managers need to consider who is doing the selling and upselling. Non-customer-facing employees are often required during times of heavy demand or staff sickness, for instance. Consideration should be given to how more customer-facing staff could be in place to cope when demands are high. Alternatively, it may mean more sales training for non-sales people so they are more aware of customer issues and concerns.

Of course, if much of your selling is done online you need to ensure, like Amazon, that you have the capability to upsell. But, the Yale research has important implications if yours is an ecommerce operation too. The research found that the level of customer satisfaction was an important factor in the likelihood of accepting an upsell. Hence if your website customers do not have a good experience, they are much less likely to opt for an automated upsell. The reason why Amazon does well in terms of upsells is because it has consistently high customer satisfaction ratings. It delivers when it says it will, it keeps you fully informed of the sales process and if things go wrong it puts them straight quickly and efficiently. If your website has slow delivery, if the site itself has functional errors, or if visitors find it hard to navigate you will have relatively low customer satisfaction and that in turn means you will have lower upsells being taken up, no matter how sophisticated the software might be. In other words, even if you have no sales people involved in upselling because it is all automated, that is not going to work unless you have highly satisfied customers.

So what are the big takeaways here?

- **Upselling depends on customer focus:** Focusing on the customer's needs and desires makes upselling more likely.
- **Focusing on targets reduces chances of upselling:** Make sure you fully understand each individual customer so that upsells become obvious. As a sales manager, provide a supportive, engaging place to work that is less focused on targets and numbers.
- **Customer satisfaction is related to upselling potential:** There is a link between customer satisfaction and the effectiveness of upselling.

Sources

Khwaja, A. & Yang, N. (2014), 'Sales Productivity and Employee Engagement: Evidence from Upselling in the Car Rental Industry'. PDF available at: nyang.sites.yale.edu/sites/default/files/EmpEngagement_KhwajaYang_29.pdf

www.smartfocus.com/blog/product-pages-should-you-cross-sell-or-sell

See also

Chapter 21 – Cross-selling works when allowed

Chapter 29 – Customers have no idea about prices

Chapter 30 – Sales promotions are for the powerless

Further reading

Schiffman, Stephan, *Upselling Techniques (That Really Work!)* (Adams Media Corporation, Avon, 2005)

www.wikihow.com/Upsell

www.problogger.net/archives/2013/04/05/mastering-the-upsell

www.creamglobal.com/search/17798/32002/do-you-want-duracell-with-that

23 POSING POWERFULLY BOOSTS NEGOTIATIONS

*Increase your confidence with special poses
and you will sell more*

Ultimately, every sale in the real world outside the Internet involves some kind of negotiation. Even at a retailer there are things that need negotiating, such as those upsells at the till, whether you will pay for a carrier bag or whether you want to be signed up to a loyalty card. The issue with negotiating, though, is that often the winner is already in a position of power before the negotiation begins.

Many sales people approach the final stages of making the sale with some trepidation because they know they now have to settle the price and the other details. They know that they are being asked to get the highest price possible and the customer, meanwhile, is trying to get the lowest price. Each side knows what the other is trying to do and they square up to one another waiting to see who will be first to crack. Little rituals take place, such as one person refusing to budge to see if they will get the other to move.

However, even though everyone involved knows what is going on, the little game carries on until they agree a truce and a compromise that both sides agree on is reached. What is commonplace, though, is that the winner is frequently the one who started out the negotiation with the highest degree of confidence. If a sales person were able to enter the negotiation phase of the sale with maximum confidence it means they would be more likely to do better out of any compromise, perhaps gaining a higher price or more favourable terms.

Research conducted at Harvard Business School looked at methods of increasing confidence prior to high pressure social situations in an interesting study conducted in 2012. This social psychology experiment wanted to see if there was a link between 'power posing' and confidence in social situations.

The researchers reasoned that in primate groups open, expansive posing is indicative of high power status in a group. Whereas closed, small poses are reflective of subservience. The researchers thought that the posing might be doing more than just sending a message about power to the other primates observing. It might well be that the poses also communicate something internally to the poser.

To put this theory to the test the psychologists had 61 male and female students from Columbia University, New York, adopt two kinds of poses while watching a computerized slide show. One group of students was asked to adopt high power poses – standing up, expansive positioning. The other group sat down and was asked to make their body small. After doing this part of the exercise the students prepared a five-minute speech as part of a job application process. The participants in the study were asked to maintain their style of posing while they prepared their talk. After they had given their speech, each student filled in a questionnaire that asked about their feelings. People who had watched the speeches were also asked to rate them and say how employable the person was.

The results were clear cut. The students who had struck the wide open, expansive power poses were judged to have performed better in their speech and were also rated the most employable. At the same time, these individuals also reported the most positive feelings after the exercise. The individuals who had adopted the constricted poses performed less well in the speech, were deemed less employable and were less likely to enjoy the experience.

Subsequent studies to this initial experiment have added some biological backing to the findings. The people who strike power poses have an increase in testosterone (in women too) at the same time as having a decrease in the stress-related hormone, cortisol.

In other words there is a hormonal change that is brought about directly as a result of adopting powerful poses, for just a few minutes.

The Harvard researchers have identified five key poses that bring about these hormonal changes, boosting confidence prior to any high stakes social situation, such as a sales negotiation.

The first pose is standing legs wide apart, just slightly further than the width of your shoulders with your hands on your hips. The next power pose is where you stand up, lean forward and plant your hands on a desk – rather like a silverback gorilla standing in front of his group. The third power pose is when you sit, leaning back in your chair, legs apart and with your hands clasped behind your head. Another sitting pose is when you sit with your legs apart and your arms outstretched on the tops of each chair either side of you. Finally, the fifth power pose is when you sit, leaning back in your chair with your feet up on the table in front of you, ankles crossed and your hands clasped behind your head.

Each of these power poses produces the hormonal changes necessary to make you feel more confident and thereby give you the edge in any sales negotiation. The standing power poses are more likely to help than the sitting ones, but each of them helps. In particular if you stand, legs apart, arms held aloft – like you have just won an Olympic race – and your hormones will adjust rapidly. Essentially, any pose that widens your stance and makes you take up more space is fairly guaranteed to make you feel more confident as a result of hormone changes; you look bigger and feel bigger.

Things to avoid that will increase your stress hormones are standing with your hands in your pockets or concealing your hands in some way. Also, if you spend time touching your face this also produces those negative stress hormones, so if you want to become a powerful negotiator, avoid such activities too.

From a practical perspective this research finding means that sales people can increase the chances they will do better out of a negotiation if they adopt power poses prior to any discussions.

That means, for example, standing up, arms wide out and pulling yourself up straight for a couple of minutes before entering any sales negotiation. If you are already in a sales meeting, taking an excuse to stand and put your hands on your hips could help. Or lean back in your chair, legs apart somewhat and your arms outstretched.

If you are on the telephone you have much greater flexibility to get yourself into the positive frame of mind and get those hormonal changes happening. You can, for instance, stand and lean on the desk while chatting hands free on the phone. Or you could lean back in your chair, arms behind your head. Indeed you can adopt such power poses when you are negotiating via email. Just lean back on your chair, feet up on the desk and your wireless keyboard on your lap; better still, get dictation software and adopt a full leaning back power pose while verbalizing your email.

Finding as many opportunities as possible for power posing is an excellent idea for sales people who want to be more confident going into any negotiation, whether face to face, on the phone or online. However, the research at Harvard showed that the posing needed several minutes to have an impact. The original study had seven minutes of posing. What this means is that just striking a pose for a few seconds is not going to be enough. You need to find time to flex those power poses for several minutes prior to any negotiation.

Don't forget too that a sales pitch is the starting point of a negotiation so power posing before you start your presentation will increase your confidence there too, making it all the more likely that people will like what you tell them.

Power posing might seem somewhat dubious, but the science is clear – your stress hormones go down and your testosterone goes up. The reverse happens when your posing is non-existent or is somewhat constricted. Stand tall and proud, take up a lot of space and you will feel good, resulting in increased confidence, thereby aiding your presentation, sales pitch or negotiation.

So what are the big takeaways here?

- **Power posing will help increase sales:** Adopting powerful poses before sales meetings make you more confident.
- **Practising power posing will help you in sales meetings:** Practise 'power posing' so that you can strike the right poses prior to sales meetings.
- **Stand up before important sales meetings to boost performance:** Sitting down immediately before an important sales presentation is likely to make you perform less well.

Source

Cuddy, Amy J. C., Wilmuth, Caroline A. & Carney, Dana R. (2012), 'The Benefit of Power Posing Before a High-Stakes Social Evaluation', Harvard Business School Working Paper, No. 13–027

Available from: nrs.harvard.edu/urn-3:HUL.InstRepos:9547823

See also

Chapter 14 – Avoid too much eye contact with customers

Chapter 16 – Selling to men or women is not the same

Chapter 18 – Get inside the mind of your buyer

Further reading

Arden, Derek, *Power Negotiating: How to Negotiate Anything, Anytime, Anywhere* (Tiptree Books, Guildford, 2010)

Neffinger, John and Kohut, Matthew, *Compelling People: The Hidden Qualities That Make Us Influential* (Piatkus, London, 2013)

www.ted.com/talks/amy_cuddy_your_body_language_shapes_who_you_are?language=en

24 COMPETITIVE SELLING NEEDS LOW PRICES

Traditional advice to start high and move down doesn't work; start low and move up

Not everything that sales people sell is at a fixed price. In many situations the sales person has the freedom to negotiate. In other situations customers are competing to buy the product or service. That can happen, for instance, in auctions, in online sales situations and when tenders are being requested. So, just how do you pitch the price when the sales situation is competitive? The fear is that if you set the price too high, you will be outbid at the lower end of the spectrum. But if you set the price too low, you could harm your profitability.

Researchers at the London Business School decided to look at this conundrum. In a series of offline and online experiments they discovered that in auctions it was better to have low initial prices rather than high ones. The study also suggested that the findings could apply in a wide range of sales situations, including when a company releases an Initial Public Offering of shares.

In the first experiment the researchers wanted to find out if the starting price in an auction had any impact on the final price paid. They said they were auctioning a US$20 bill. Two groups of students were asked to say how many bids (in US$1 increments) they would make and when they would stop bidding. One group was set a starting price of US$1, whereas the other group had a starting bid of US$10. The results showed that more bids were made by the group of participants who had started out at US$1 and that these bids also led to a final higher price offered than was the case for the group who started out at US$10. To some extent this is counterintuitive. Setting a low starting price sets an 'anchor' in the minds of the participants as to the value of what they were bidding on. A low anchor price means people perceive the item to be of lower value. This is why many people setting prices in online auctions, for instance, do not want to set low starting prices because it devalues what they are offering. Yet, this experiment showed that concern to be false. It demonstrated that lower starting prices led to a higher final price being paid than was the case when starting prices were closer to the actual value of the item being offered.

In a second experiment, the London Business School, cooperating with a team at Northwestern University in Illinois, looked at whether or not the low starting price in an auction did indeed lead to a sense of lower value. Participants were asked to imagine they were looking at a shirt for sale on eBay. One group of participants was told the starting price was US$1, the other group was told the starting price was US$24.99. Each group was asked to estimate the actual value of the shirt. They were also asked to say how many bids they would make before deciding to give up on bidding. This was to find out what the maximum price people would pay for the item.

The results of this experiment found that – as in the previous experiment – the low starting price led to more bids being made. It also showed that people valued the shirt at much less when it was at a starting price of US$1 than the people who were told the shirt was starting at US$24.99. This makes sense – if the starting price is low, people value the item more cheaply than if the starting price is high. However, when the starting price was high there were fewer bids and less movement on price than was the case for the low starting price. In other words, even though people in the US$1 starting price group valued the shirt lower than the US$24.99 group, more of them bid and the resulting price paid was significantly more than the starting price. Just because a price anchor makes people value an item more, it does not mean they are going to pay for it. They appear more willing to pay – and end up paying more – if the anchor price is low and they value the item less.

To further explore this intriguing result, the researchers looked at actual auction data from eBay. They looked at two completely different product areas – Nikon cameras and Persian rugs. These were chosen because they are both highly priced items which have high perceived value. Furthermore, they both attract a lot of activity on eBay. A total of 266 different auctions were included in the analysis.

The data showed that when the starting price was low, the auction was much more likely to be completed than when the starting price was high. Also, items with lower starting prices had more bids and more unique bidders than items that started high. It seems that the lower starting prices encouraged more bidding activity, leading to a higher end price than was the case for items that started with a high initial price.

In yet more analysis the researchers wanted to find out why this might be happening. They looked at bids made on mid-price shirts sold by the same company. Like many other sellers on eBay this company offered the same items in different listings, with some listings at low starting prices and others at a higher starting price. Being able to compare activity on such listings led the London Business School researchers to find out why the lower price items tend to get more bids and a final higher price.

It turns out that when the starting price is low and people are making more bids their 'costs' are higher. They are having to spend more time, have to bid more frequently and have to monitor what is going on. This means they have invested more in the item from a psychological perspective and that could explain why they stick with the bidding process and why, therefore, more people doing more of that leads to higher final prices. It appears that the increase in final sale price is due to the desire to recoup the time investment made in the bidding process.

But what about the value people place on items in competitive selling situations? This is a clear worry on the part of sales people. You might be able to start low, but if that devalues what you are selling, what is the point? This was another notion that the researchers put to the test. They asked people to bid on a holiday. One group of participants had a low starting price and the other group had a high starting price. As in the previous experiments, the low starting price led to more activity and a higher final price. But this study found that the additional activity in the low starting price group led them to re-evaluate the value they had placed on the holiday. The amount of bidding made them think it was more valuable than their original estimates. Far from low starting prices making people undervalue what you are selling, it can – in specific situations – make them reconsider their valuation and increase their original notion.

This set of experiments from the London Business School and Northwestern University provides a fascinating insight into the buying process in competitive situations, such as an eBay auction. However, as the researchers themselves point out, the findings can be extended to many other competitive sales scenarios. Not every sales encounter is dealing with fixed prices. Sometimes buyers are in competition with each other. You might have a limited supply of products or service availability, for instance. Or you may be in competition with other sellers in a bidding process for a tender.

In such situations it is counterintuitive to start with a low price. Yet as this research shows, starting low leads to a high final price. Sales people often have three prices for competitive situations – the maximum price they would love to get, the price they think they can probably get and their lowest possible price below which they will not accept any offers. Generally, people start high knowing they'll be brought down somewhere near to the middle-ground price they were thinking of. But this research suggests that starting lower could end up in a final higher price, if you can inject competition for the buyer into the process. You can do this by making your product scarce, or in high demand from many other people, for example. You could say that you'll sell the items at £5 each, but they are rarely available and you have ten other customers who also want them. You'll then find that the prospect is willing to pay £7 to secure the items for themselves. If you had started at £8 they might had driven you down to £5.

Starting low is not the big risk that many sales people might think. In competitive situations, starting low could be the answer to increasing your profits by increasing the likelihood of a final sale at a higher price.

So what are the big takeaways here?

- **Prices prime customer expectations:** The first price you mention determines the final price you get.
- **Start with low prices when competing:** In competitive situations, start with a lower price than you might think sensible. It will lead to a higher final price.
- **People spend more if entry price is low:** People are encouraged to spend more when the initial price reduces the barrier to entry in the competition.

Source

Ku, G., Galinsky, A. D. & Murnighan, J. K. (2006) 'Starting Low but Ending High: A Reversal of the Anchoring Effect in Auctions', *Journal of Personality and Social Psychology*, Vol. 90 No. 6 pp 975–86

See also

Chapter 20 – Closing sales is not necessary

Chapter 25 – Kindness kills objections

Chapter 30 – Sales promotions are for the powerless

Further reading

Chase, Landy, *Competitive Selling: Out-Plan, Out-Think, Out-Sell to Win Every Time* (McGraw-Hill Books, Columbus, 2010)

Hunter, Mark, *High-Profit Selling: Win the Sale Without Compromising on Price* (AMACOM, New York, 2012)

25 KINDNESS KILLS OBJECTIONS

Being nice to your customers is all it takes to get them to forget objections to buying

Every sales person worries about objections. You get all the way through a sales appointment but at the back of your mind the whole time is 'what will they raise as an objection?' Sales trainers say that when running training courses the session on 'handling objections' is the one that generates the most interest and interaction. Sales people are dominated by the desire to deal with inevitable objections.

It is, though, a needless worry. Objections only happen when you have not provided the right information in the right way and when you have failed to do your homework so that you can quote the right price for that specific customer. If you have researched them well, provided the information the way they want it and set the price at their expected level, there is almost nothing for a prospect to object to.

Even so, objections are part and parcel of everyday life for sales people, so researchers at the College of Business and Public Administration, Old Dominion University, Norfolk, Virginia, decided to investigate the topic. They enrolled 116 couples who were seeking life insurance into the study and then actually studied 100 of them. Their encounters with life insurance sales people were video recorded for analysis. In addition, prior to the sales meeting they filled in questionnaires that helped the researchers discover their preferred buying style. After the sales appointment each couple also filled in a further questionnaire that determined their level of satisfaction with the sales person.

Each video-recorded appointment was divided into phases and the way the sales person handled objections was also coded. The video was divided into three phases, the first of which was judged to be about building credibility with the customer, with the remaining two phases when objections were raised. In terms of analysing those objections, the coding was divided into two kinds. One style of handling objections was about delivering expertise, the other was called the benevolence style, whereby the sales person simply offered kindness and support, rather than trying to prove the company really could help.

A total of 72 different objections were raised by the couples involved in the study. The two different styles of handling those objections were used in roughly equal measure by the sales people. However, in the first phase of the analysis, when the sales people were trying to build credibility, most of what they said was in the 'expertise' category, rather than 'benevolence'. For instance, an 'expertise' credibility statement might be along the lines of a sales person saying how much experience they have in the world of life assurance. However, a 'benevolence' statement would be when the sales person asked how they could help the couple. Expertise statements are focused on the company, benevolence statements are focused on the buyer.

The researchers had previously asked the participants for information in a questionnaire that revealed their buying style. So they could now see if there was any connection between the objection-handling and their buying style. The results showed that there were three main kinds of buying style. The first style was an interactive style, where the customers spent a lot of time chatting and socializing with the salesperson. The second style was where the customers were focused on the task in hand of getting the required information. There was a third type of buying style where the customers were completely self-focused and did not talk much about the products.

What became clear in this research was that the buying style was linked to the kind of credibility statements that worked the best. People with an interactive style responded more positively to the benevolence statements. However, people who had a task-oriented style responded best to expertise statements. There were no significant findings for the third buying style.

The study also showed that most of the credibility building was done in the first third of the sales encounter. After that, objections started to arise and so the researchers were keen to find out if there was a link between the ways those objections were handled and the buying style of the customer. What they discovered was fascinating. The sales people were clearly good at detecting the buying style of the customer. When a customer responded positively in the first phase of the meeting to either an expertise or benevolence statement, the sales person used more of those kinds of words and phrases – clearly trying to 'fit in' with the requirements of the individuals. However, when it came to the objection phase of the analysis it was discovered that responding in the way the sales person had 'learned' was good for the customer but did not subsequently work. In other words, people respond differently according to the sales phase they are in.

When people are in the first phase of buying they expect the sales person to respond in the style that fits with them. But the study showed that when it comes to the objections phase of the appointment people who previously reacted positively to expertise statements no longer responded to them. The researchers found that in terms of objection-handling customers respond to benevolence statements regardless of their buying style or what they had reacted to positively in the initial phase of the sale.

The study is clear – when people raise objections the crucial thing to do is to be kind to them, see things from their perspective and avoid trying to 'prove' your product or service is what they really want. Regardless of a customer's buying style it appears that the most effective way of handling objections is simply being nice to them.

From a practical perspective this has several benefits. It means that instead of having to learn any fancy techniques to deal with objections you just have to be that nice, kind, normal person you are. You then just have to react to those objections by being 'human'. That also means that during any sales encounter you can stop worrying about what the objections might be and concentrate on truly connecting with the customer, thereby boosting the relationship. Another benefit is that sales managers do not have to spend money and waste sales team time on going on 'objection handling' training courses that try to teach 'techniques' or 'tricks' to deal with objections.

The research also means that sales people need to be aware of what phase in the buying process they are in. Has the appointment moved from the initial phase through to the questioning or objection phase? The research clearly showed that sales people need to change their behaviour according to the phase of the encounter. During that first phase a sales person needs to detect the buying style of the customer and respond appropriately, with expertise statements for instance. But when the appointment switches to the objection phase, the sales person needs to switch to benevolence mode, regardless of the type of customer.

Clearly this means that sales people need to be constantly aware of the appointment and have to listen actively to what the customer is saying. Only by listening fully and actively can you detect when the encounter is moving from that initial phase into objections. At that point you need to switch your behaviour into full-on benevolence.

However, you can also make sure that you are on the right pathway for the customer buying style in advance. During the discussion of the study the researchers pointed out that other studies had shown that buying styles are linked to advertising, branding, word of mouth and so on, which all set the expectations of the customer. That means thinking about the way the company communicates with customers and how they perceive that allows you to reasonably predict the kind of buying style you will meet. Advanced preparation like this and thinking about the perspective of the customer means you are likely to have fewer objections anyway, but those you do get you'll be able to respond to more effectively because you will be seeing things much more from the customer's perspective. That will enable you to come across in a much more kind way, reducing the impact of those objections.

So what are the big takeaways here?

- **Kindness is more important than expertise:** Being kind and saying nice things is more likely to help you overcome sales objections than showing you are the experts.
- **Being a good listener is important in sales:** Prepare for sales meetings and listen to what your customers are saying.
- **Your brand and your competitors influence how people buy:** The buying style of your customers that you have to fit in with is determined by your company's advertising and brand presence as well as that of your competitors.

Source

Arndt, A., Evans, K., Landry, T. D., Mady, S. & Pongpatipat, C. (2014), 'The impact of salesperson credibility-building statements on later stages of the sales encounter', *Journal of Personal Selling & Sales Management*, Vol. 34 Issue 1 pp 19–32

See also

Chapter 1 – Consultative selling is expected

Chapter 11 – Persistence pays in sales

Chapter 18 – Get inside the mind of your buyer

Chapter 28 – Perfect pitches come from mood setting

Further reading

Farber, Barry, *Handling Sales Objections: Win more deals* (Crimson Business, Richmond, 2009)

www.wikihow.com/Handle-Sales-Objections

26 MINDFULNESS CAN CUT CONFLICT

Be 'in the moment' and stop thinking
if you want to get more sales

Plenty of sales people behave in a 'mindful' way, without realizing they are using 'mindfulness'. Being mindful means you are present, fully, in the here and now, paying complete attention to what is happening around you and not distracted by anything. Sales people who do this are not thinking about the impending objections, nor are they concerning themselves with ticking off something on a target list. Instead, they are just focusing on the customer and thinking of nothing else.

Meanwhile, there are sales people who are so concerned with their targets, or thinking of which 'sales close' technique they ought to be using, that they have lost any true connection with the customer. Indeed, they have often not really heard what the customer is saying to them. They are not 'present' because their mind is elsewhere. If their mind is elsewhere, how can they effectively respond to the customer?

Most of the work on mindfulness has been in the personal development arena. Increasingly, though, it is being seen as a useful business tool. It can help meetings at work go more smoothly, for instance, and it can help people work together more effectively on projects together. There is also the notion that companies themselves can be mindful. This happens when the organization is constantly aware of its marketplace and what its customers and suppliers are doing or saying. Corporate mindfulness happens when the entire business is completely aware of its stakeholders.

Given that mindfulness seems to be a bit 'new age' or somewhat 'soft', the more hard-nosed sales managers might not consider this as something worthy of their attention. However, growing amounts of research are pointing to the value of a mindful approach in business.

One such study comes from the Griffith Business School from Queensland, Australia, which investigated the relationship between mindfulness and the use of healthcare services in Malaysia. The researchers wanted to find out whether satisfaction with healthcare was related in any way to mindfulness.

They looked at the reliability of care, the way conflict was handled, and the reliability of information and the connection between these factors and customer satisfaction. The investigators also looked at the link between these aspects of care and the loyalty the users had to the particular supplier.

Mindfulness theory suggests that factors such as reliability of care in a healthcare setting can only truly take place if the carer has listened to the precise needs of the patient. Similarly, without being mindful of the individual patient's needs it would not be possible for the information passed on to be reliable. As a result, the researchers believed that there would be a link between mindfulness and favourable ratings on things like customer satisfaction.

To find out if this were the case 423 consumers of healthcare in Kuala Lumpur were asked to complete a detailed questionnaire. The participants were users of ten different healthcare organizations. The details of the questionnaire were then analysed and several statistical tests completed. What the researchers discovered was that customer satisfaction was significantly related to the reliability of care, the reliability of information and the way conflict was handled. In particular what was called 'pre-emptive' conflict handling was important. In other words, when the staff were behaving in a truly mindful way they were able to prevent conflict from happening to a large degree.

This is one of the first large studies that has shown a clear connection between mindfulness and outcomes. Customer satisfaction was directly linked to mindful behaviours, showing that when the hospitals and the staff were so present 'in the moment' with their healthcare consumers the satisfaction ratings were at their highest.

There are several implications of this study for those working in sales. Sales people are always told to try to see things from the perspective of the customer and to empathize with them. Often, though, this is not possible. Simple things like being a male sales assistant in a female clothing shop means that no matter how hard the man tries he cannot fully empathize with the women customers. Similarly, a pharmaceutical sales representative cannot truly see things from the perspective of a consultant cardiac surgeon customer, even though they understand something of what they do. Empathy and seeing things from the perspective of the customer is excellent, of course, but it is not always possible.

Mindfulness, however, is more than empathy and seeing things from the perspective of the customer. Hence from a sales perspective it can be a significant addition to a sales person's ability to truly connect with their customers. With increased connection and understanding it is possible to reduce conflict, the research showed. Sales people who practise mindfulness are therefore more likely to gain sales as well as less likely to engage in any kind of conflict with customers.

The trouble is, most of us are not mindful. We face too many distractions and thoughts that prevent us from being 'in the moment'. However, it is perfectly possible to learn mindfulness and then become more mindful in all your sales encounters as a result.

One way of doing this is to take an 'improv' class. Actors and comedians learn the skills of improvisation and the only way they can make these unrehearsed and unscripted scenes work for an audience is to be 'in the moment'. Unless the actors are completely immersed in the moment, listening fully and not distracted by anything whatsoever, then the scene fails to work. The best improv actors and comedians are those who live in that moment. Everything else is irrelevant to them. Taking an improv class can significantly increase your ability to be 'in the moment'.

You can also help improve your mindfulness by noticing those moments you normally ignore, such as when you are brushing your teeth. Many of us clean our teeth and listen to the radio at the same time, or we just think about the problems of the day ahead. We are rarely fully aware of our teeth-brushing moment. By concentrating and paying attention to brushing your teeth every morning, you soon get used to being 'in the moment' and can use that skill in a sales scenario, helping you absorb everything about your customer.

Finding any reason to be mindful, even for a few moments, can help you become more mindful generally. Try to be 'in the moment' when waiting for a train or when in the queue at the supermarket. The more chances you take to pay attention to everything around you at tiny moments each day, the more mindful you will become naturally.

Having increased your ability to be mindful you can then use it in sales situations. This will help you pay extremely close attention to everything that is going on. You will be able to provide more of the right information, more of the necessary details and more of the answers the customer is seeking. As the research from Malaysia shows, when you do this you increase customer satisfaction at the same time as reducing the potential for any conflict.

So what are the big takeaways here?

- **Stop thinking and be present:** Being present 'in the moment' reduces conflict and increases the likelihood of sales.
- **Learn mindfulness to boost sales:** Learn mindfulness techniques or just focus on paying attention to the customer and listening to what they say.
- **Concentrate on the present to be more mindful:** Mindfulness is not complicated. All it takes is concentrating on the here and now.

Source

Ndubisi, N.O. (2012), 'Mindfulness, reliability, pre-emptive conflict handling, customer orientation and outcomes in Malaysia's healthcare sector', *Journal of Business Research*, Vol. 65 Issue 4 pp 537–46

See also

Chapter 16 – Selling to men or women is not the same

Chapter 18 – Get inside the mind of your buyer

Chapter 25 – Kindness kills objections

Further reading

Alidina, Shamash and Adams, Juliet, *Mindfulness at Work For Dummies* (John Wiley & Sons, Chichester, 2014)

Cremer, John, *Improv* (Sunmakers, Oxford, 2011)

Gunn, Jane, *How to Beat Bedlam in the Boardroom and Boredom in the Bedroom* (Corporate Peacemakers, Reading, 2011)

blog.pipedrive.com/2013/04/mindfulness-and-sales-results

27 COLD CALLS WEAKEN SALES

Meet customers in the real world, then
call them if you want to sell on the phone

There are more ways to reach customers and to sell to them than ever before. In the past you could write to them, meet them in the real world or phone them. Once the fax was invented that introduced another way of selling to people. Then along came email, websites, instant messaging, text messages, social networks and a host of other ways of reaching customers directly. Yet in spite of this massive expansion in the ability to contact customers and promote something to them, the humble telephone appears remarkably resilient as a selling tool. Far from cold calling on the phone becoming less attractive to sales people, because of all the other options, it seems to be gaining popularity.

Research from the London School of Economics shows that cold calling is an increasing problem. In the space of the three years up to 2013 the number of complaints about cold calls made to the regulators went up more than five-fold. Indeed, BT alone receives 50,000 complaints about cold calls every month.

The Information Commissioner in the UK has investigated cold calling issues and found that the bulk of the problems about which people complain comes specifically from the automated calls. These are cold calls where a recorded message is played or sometimes where there is no sound at all, as the system is merely checking to see if someone answers the phone. Cold calls from a real person represent only about 20 per cent of the complaints. Even so, that is tens of thousands of complaints about unwanted cold calls.

Almost every sales person dreads making cold calls. You need a thick skin and the ability to cope with rejection most of the time. You also have to be able to ignore the negativity or downright rudeness coming at you from the person you have called. The success rate of cold calls is pitifully low – yet most businesses make them, because they always have done. Indeed, according to Which? from the Consumers' Association, 70 per cent of people they surveyed receive cold calls. Sales people may dislike cold calling, but they certainly do a lot of it!

Research by Mahan Khalsa from the consultancy firm Franklin Covey found that completely cold calls only had a success rate in terms of gaining an appointment of less than 3 per cent, with many companies achieving only a 0.1 per cent success rate. However, when calls were made following a referral, the success rate went up significantly. If a sales person is referred by an internal source – one person in a business recommending the sales person to a colleague – then the success rate is 82 per cent. If the referral is from an outsider – someone known to the potential customer but who does not work for the business – the success rate is 44 per cent. The same level of success happens when the call follows a meeting with the customer, such as at an exhibition or a business networking event. The Franklin Covey research confirmed what many sales people know instinctively – cold calling is a huge waste of their time. Research published in *American Banker* magazine, though, shows that cold calling takes up about 20 per cent of a sales person's time.

In addition to the timewasting nature of cold calling, there are the inevitable negative consequences of annoying prospects and being considered a nuisance. The data from the regulators such as Ofcom revealed by the London School of Economics show that people are having decreasing patience with cold calling. If you cold call, you are not only annoying yourself because of all the rejection and negativity, but you are also putting off potential customers.

In an attempt to find out how cold calling really affects people, researchers at the Jaipuria Institute of Management, India, investigated the attitudes of 400 individuals from two different cities, Lucknow and Kanpur in Uttar Pradesh, in the north of the country. All 400 people were interviewed using a structured questionnaire.

The researchers found that there was a clear relationship between positive attitudes to cold calling and the degree to which the individuals could get a 'deal' that was personally interesting to them. In other words, if the call was specific and relevant, the attitudes towards it were more positive. Although some people were positive towards telemarketing generally, this was a factor mediated by the likelihood of getting a personally relevant deal. Even if people were not unduly annoyed by cold calls, the likelihood of purchase was only present if the cold call was specific to the person receiving it.

Privacy concerns were a significant issue for the 400 people in the study. This was one of the key reasons for lack of any subsequent purchase. Lack of trust of cold callers was a real issue.

These research results, together with the findings from Franklin Covey, show that cold calling has extremely limited potential. In spite of sales people spending one fifth of their time conducting cold calls, it seems there is very little point in doing it. What these findings demonstrate is that cold calling wastes time and produces few sales. However 'warm calling' does lead to sales.

One form of 'warm calling' is to phone someone who already knows you or to whom you have been recommended. The second form of 'warm calling' – revealed by the Indian research – is to people who you have done your homework on and consequently you know exactly what they want. You can dramatically increase the chances of sales from telemarketing if you ensure you either phone people who you know want what you are offering, or you call people who you have been told are expecting your call because you have been recommended to them.

The first thing you can do to increase the chances of cold calls working is to attend more business networking events, conferences, exhibitions and so on where you can meet likely customers. You can use such events to find out more specifically about the potential for doing business with the individuals you meet. Importantly, ask them for their permission to call them and get a specific day when it would be best to phone them. You can then part from these individuals saying 'I'll look forward to speaking with you on the phone on Tuesday morning'. When you do call on Tuesday morning it is no longer a cold call, but a warm one because the person you met is expecting you to ring. They have also given you permission to call, so if you are met by a gatekeeper on the phone you can legitimately say that the person you are calling is expecting your call following your meeting.

Another way of being able to generate 'warm calls' is to ask your existing contacts within a company to nominate who else in the firm is likely to want the kind of products and services you sell. You might, for instance, be supplying one particular division or team within a company yet there could be other groups in the business who could use your services. Ask your contact to recommend you – give them some leaflets or business cards they can pass on. Also, ask your contact if you can call in a few days' time to ask who showed an interest when your details were passed on. That way you have permission to call your contact again, plus it gives them a bit of a push to actually pass on your name. When you call your contact you can then find out the names of the people to whom you were recommended. Then, when you call them, they are a warm lead and it won't be a cold call.

Referrals and warm calls, however, are not always going to be enough to generate the required numbers of leads and sales. So sometimes you will have to call people who have no idea who you are. However, as the Indian research showed, people are receptive to telemarketing calls as long as those calls offer precisely what they want. This means that you can generate business from cold calls if you have done sufficient customer research in advance. If you are selling in a B2B sense this is relatively easy because the company will have a website, it will be well represented on LinkedIn and you will be able to find out a great deal of information to help you target specific people with particular interests. In the B2C sector this is more difficult – however, many individuals have social media profiles that can help you understand whether they might be amenable to buying. Indeed, social media advertising uses data from the words they type and the kinds of things they click on to deliver targeted promotions to them. You can do much the same, perhaps even contacting people using social media and then gaining their permission to call them in the future.

Whichever way you decide to go, though, the research is clear – cold calling is a mug's game, but appropriate phone calls to the right people can lead to significant sales.

So what are the big takeaways here?

- **Forget cold calls:** Cold calling wastes time. Warm calling leads to sales.
- **More sales come from getting out and about:** Get out and meet more customers at exhibitions and networking events. Get referrals so you can call people who already know about you and your company.
- **Permission marketing works:** Your phone calls to prospects are much more likely to succeed if they have already given you permission to call them and if you are referred to them. Cold calling is unlikely to work.

Sources

Agarwal, R. & Mehrotra, A. (2009), 'Telemarketing – a bane or a boon for companies? An assessment of Indian customers' attitude and perception towards telemarketing', *Journal of Customer Behaviour*, Autumn 2009, Vol. 8 Issue 3 pp 257–91

Milne, C. (2013), 'Nuisance calls: a case for concerted action', LSE Media Policy Project Series, Broughton Micova, Sally and Tambini, Damian (eds.) Media Policy Brief 8. London School of Economics and Political Science, London, UK

American Banker (2006), Vol. 171 Issue 35, p 2

See also

Chapter 3 – Direct selling still succeeds

Chapter 12 – How to find prospects

Chapter 30 – Sales promotions are for the powerless

Further reading

Godin, Seth, *Permission Marketing* (Pocket Books, London, 2007)

Khalsa, Mahan, *Let's Get Real or Let's Not Play: Transforming the Buyer/Seller Relationship* (Penguin, New York, 2008)

Rumbauskas, Frank J. Jr, *Never Cold Call Again: Achieve Sales Greatness without Cold Calling* (Wiley, New Jersey, 2006)

salesperformance.franklincovey.com/insights

28 PERFECT PITCHES COME FROM MOOD SETTING

*Make your customers happy and relaxed
and they are more likely to buy*

At some stage sales people have to pitch. In B2B settings this can be quite formal, with a slide presentation, for example. In situations where a tender is being applied for the formality can increase with a team presentation being supported by extensive documentation, sometimes running into hundreds of pages. At the other end of the pitching extreme comes the informal pitch made by a retail sales assistant, encouraging a shopper to buy a particular item. Whichever specific situation a sales person is in, pitching is inevitable.

A pitch can win or lose the business, so it is no surprise that sales people are sent on a wide array of training courses. Sales people attend courses on everything from how to write pitches to presentation skills and dealing with the nervousness of standing in front of a panel of customers. Pitching and presenting is among the most concerning part of working in sales. Sales people become extremely nervous and tense when having to present. Indeed, in some studies the fear of doing presentations has been rated as higher than the fear of spiders or heights – even death...!

The fear of doing pitches is created by two main concerns. First, the individual feels 'in the spotlight' and is therefore open to judgement on the way they are doing the pitch, their personal appearance and so on. Second, the sales person who has to do a pitch is concerned that they might not get the sale. Two pressures like this combine to make sales pitches one of the most worrying parts of a sales person's job.

The problem with these worries about doing pitches is that all the focus of sales training is on the person who has to make the presentation. Even though the training may emphasize the need to 'focus on the audience' the whole point of the training is to ensure that the sales person feels good about pitching.

Research conducted at the University of Alabama, though, suggests it is vital to consider how the customer feels prior to the pitch, if you want the sale to be more likely to succeed. This research shows that the mood of your customer has a significant impact on whether or not they are likely to buy from you.

The study involved 182 participants who were recruited having been told they were needed for two different pieces of research. This was a ploy because the two pieces were connected. The first element of the study involved people being asked to watch a video and give some comments about it. According to the researchers who briefed the participants, the videos were being considered for viewing at an event at the university and they were seeking reactions to the potential videos before deciding which one to show. Some people were shown a humorous video, others were shown a straight documentary. The videos were not being selected for showing at an event, of course. This was just the story the participants were told. The funny video was being used to put some participants into a good, positive mood. The straight documentary had been designed to be unlikely to alter the mood of the participants, keeping them relatively neutral.

As soon as the video was over the participants were then introduced to a second researcher, supposedly doing another experiment on the suitability of a sales presentation. Some of the participants were told at this point that the sales presenter was an intern who was seeing if the job was suitable. The other group of participants was told that the presentation was being made by someone who needed just one more sale in order to reach their target. This meant that there were four categories of people in the study:

1. Happy people who thought the sales person had no ulterior motive (the intern)

2. Neutral mood people who thought the sales person had no ulterior motive
3. Happy people who thought the sales person did have an ulterior motive (meeting the target)
4. Neutral mood people who thought the sales person had an ulterior motive.

The study was designed to find out if there was a relationship between mood, perceived ulterior motives and the level of sales and presentation skills that the participant attributed to the sales person. The researchers also performed a further experiment to see if there was any relationship between the mood of the potential buyer and their likelihood of buying.

The results demonstrated that there was indeed a relationship between the mood of the participants and their views of the sales person. When people had been placed into a good mood as a result of the funny video they rated the sales person's skills more highly and disregarded the supposed ulterior motive. However, the people in a neutral mood after watching the documentary focused on the ulterior motive and also rated the presentational skills less favourably. The study also found that when the sales presentation was strong and people were in a good mood the purchase intention was high.

These findings have important implications for sales people. They suggest that it is the prior mood of the buyers before the presentation begins that is one of the greatest predictors of the likelihood of sales success. If a customer is in a good mood prior to the sales pitch they are more likely to buy and are less likely to pick out the negative features, such as the motivation of the sales person. However, if a customer is in a neutral mood, the research shows that they are more likely to notice the motivations of the sales person, unless their presentation is particularly strong.

For many sales people this research means they ought to find ways of boosting the mood of the customers prior to the pitch or presentation. You could consider the use of background music, for instance, prior to the presentation. Similarly, you could let them watch a funny video before your presentation actually begins – some kind of humorous scene-setter. Performing a sales pitch in the right environment is also worth thinking about if you wish to set a positive mood. Are your premises mood-enhancing for instance? Or should you choose somewhere more positive?

Sometimes you cannot manipulate the environment because you have to present at the customer's premises. Equally, you might be part of a 'beauty parade' with competing suppliers pitching before you. As a result the mood of the customer is set by the people who pitched before you. In these situations you need to be able to lighten the mood before you make your presentation somehow. This is where a humorous video may come in useful, or perhaps you could start your presentation with a couple of scene-setting cartoons. Clearly, what you do has to be appropriate to the customer and the circumstances, but prior to any pitch you ought to consider how you can help create a positive mood at the beginning.

By creating a good mood among your customers you are much more likely to get the sale and you lessen the chances they will spot your ulterior motives. Even if they do, the research shows they are forgiving. Even so, you may not be able to lighten the mood as much as you wish. The research suggests that there is only one way out of this: you need to have a strong, customer-focused pitch. For neutral mood customers just trotting out the same old PowerPoint® presentation is not good enough; they will see right through the ploy. Instead, you need something that is strongly linked to the specific requirements of that customer. Even though they may see your motivation for the sales pitch, a strong customer-centric presentation makes up for it. In short, if you adapt your pitch to the specific requirements of the customer who is in a neutral mood you will probably change their mood into a positive one.

Worrying about your nerves, concentrating on developing great slides, getting your wording right – are all things that many sales presenters focus on. However, the Alabama research shows that one of the best things you can do is to get your customers in the right mood. If you can't boost their positive mood, then make sure everything you talk about in your presentation is about them.

So what are the big takeaways here?

- **Make your customers smile:** Happy customers are not suspicious of sales people.
- **Don't start selling until customers are positive:** Boost your presentation skills so that every pitch puts your customers in a positive mood.
- **Avoid selling when customers are not positive:** If customers remain in a neutral mood they become suspicious of the motives of a sales person, thereby reducing the likely impact of the sales presentation.

Source

DeCarlo, T. E. & Barone, M. J. (2013), 'The Interactive Effects of Sales Presentation, Suspicion, and Positive Mood on Salesperson Evaluations and Purchase Intentions', *Journal of Personal Selling & Sales Management*, Vol. 33 Issue 1 pp 53–66

See also

Chapter 2 – Adaptive selling is vital

Chapter 9 – Key accounts need knowledge

Chapter 19 – Spotting those buying signals

Chapter 25 – Kindness kills objections

Further reading

Davies, Graham, *The Presentation Coach* (Capstone, Chichester, 2010)

Lopata, Andy and Roper, Peter, *... and Death Came Third!: The Definitive Guide to Networking and Speaking in Public* (Ecademy Press, St Albans, 2011)

Pink, Daniel H., *To Sell Is Human: The Surprising Truth About Persuading, Convincing, and Influencing Others* (Canongate Books, New York, 2014)

Vincent, Jack, *Sales Pitches that Snap, Crackle 'n Pop* (Brave New Sales, Ocean City, 2012)

29 CUSTOMERS HAVE NO IDEA ABOUT PRICES

People find it hard to assess cost, but they can estimate value

At some point in a sales conversation the customer is going to ask 'how much?' But they are not really asking you to tell them the price. In many sales encounters sales people worry about quoting the price as they fear it will sound too costly. Yet the price is just a series of numbers that are largely meaningless to the buyer. This was established in a series of studies from two psychologists, Daniel Kahneman and Amos Tversky. Their work was so important that Kahneman received a Nobel Prize for his research and Tversky was posthumously mentioned by the Nobel Committee. This posthumous mention was an extraordinary event, confirming the significance of the work done by these two scientists.

What they discovered was that the actual value of something – whether that is in monetary terms or some other measurement, such as time – is less important in our decision-making than what we might lose by having it or not having it. Kahneman and Tversky were able to discover that 'loss aversion' is what drives us to make decisions. It is, essentially, part of our human survival mechanism that ensures we avoid risky losses. Part of that system also looks at whether or not we are going to gain something.

When we are deciding to buy something we are calculating whether we will lose something by purchasing it, or lose something if we do not buy it. At the same time, our brain is busy working out what we might gain if we buy the item and what we might gain by not purchasing it. The actual price itself appears to be only a small factor in this mental calculation. The most important psychological factor when we buy something is the aversion to loss.

Yet, while their customers are busy worrying about the risks they might be taking and the associated losses, sales people are focused on the actual numbers of the price, concerning themselves that they might seem too expensive, or worse, too cheap. Once more in the world of sales, the sales person and the customer are looking at the transaction from completely different perspectives.

Another factor identified by Tversky was the issue of perceived value. When a company has an item for sale, say at £100, it might seem too highly priced because customers do not perceive it has having that kind of value, in comparison to other items at the same price, or compared with other similar items at different prices. In this instance the loss aversion calculation kicks in and the potential customer focuses on the loss of the cash, rather than the gain of the item.

However, if the company selling the item at £100 were now to introduce a similar enhanced version at, say, £200, the original item no longer looks expensive. Indeed, compared with the higher-priced version it now seems good value. The loss aversion rule now applies to the higher-priced item, making the lower-priced one seem attractive. Many companies introduce high-priced items that they do not really intend selling very much of at all. They are merely there to ensure that the item they really want to sell is then perceived as good value by the customers. Had the lower-priced item been the only one available, fewer sales would be made.

This feature of pricing and the consideration of value was studied by researchers in New Zealand when they asked 250 people to answer one of three questionnaires that were looking at prices and values. People were asked questions about what they would pay to buy particular items and were given price choices from a list.

The researchers discovered that the price people would be prepared to pay was affected by how many different price points were mentioned, whether those prices were in ascending or descending order and how far apart the prices were – the spread of the amounts. Like other studies, the research confirmed that people were prepared to pay more when there were additional prices listed and when these prices were much higher than the desired item. When a range of prices for a variety of items is provided, people tend to aim higher and choose to buy things at a higher price. For instance, if you had an item for sale at £10 and offered three versions at £8, £10 and £12, many people would opt for the £10 item. However, if you offered alternatives at £8, £10, £12 and £20, many more people would decide to buy the £12 item. Simply listing an item at a much higher price can cause people to opt to buy an item that would otherwise be perceived as too costly. It is not the actual cost people are measuring when making such judgements, but relative perceived losses.

Another factor in how customers judge prices is how they perceive the price itself. When the sales person puts the price and the actual numerical value as the frame of reference, the customer will make comparisons based on that number. However, when the sales person (or the web page, for that matter) uses a frame of reference that is not based on the price, the customer determines gains and losses on that framing. This means that sales people can compare and contrast features and benefits and point out the losses of not opting for the item with most features.

The research into the psychology of prices throws up a wide array of complications. However, central to most findings is the concept of the losses that people prefer to avoid. These are the factors that people focus on more than the actual price. Indeed, the research shows that once people have decided to buy, getting even more money out of them is comparatively easy because now they do not wish to lose the item they have bought.

For most sales people all of these research findings mean one key thing: stop worrying about the actual price, because your customers are not bothered about it that much. Instead, focusing discussions on what customers could lose by not buying is a productive way to go. For instance, imagine selling a dishwasher. Customers might focus on the loss of the £250 that is being charged, but the sales person can shift this focus to the loss of time with the family as a result of spending time doing the washing-up by hand. At the same time the customer can also be focused on the gain of time with children. If next to the

£250 dishwasher there is another similar one for £400, the loss of the £250 becomes small in comparison to the loss of time with the family.

In most sales presentations it is possible to address the potential losses that customers will have as a result of not buying. Furthermore, it is generally possible to have each item you sell listed together with other similar but more expensive items. If you do not have a series of prices for similar items, that is something worth producing. Companies will find sales increase when they present price ranges, instead of having one item at a fixed price point. Customers have no means of comparison and can only focus on the loss of their cash at that point. With other prices for similar items available, they can be focused on the losses of not buying and they then see the increased value in the item you are really trying to sell them.

Focusing the mind of the buyer on other factors is a key feature when you are selling online. Use features and benefits lists and have comparative lists showing how each tier of product or service differs. Also, comparing yourself to the features offered by the competition puts people's minds into concerning themselves with the losses of not buying from you. The price can then be a small feature in design terms because by the time people have realized they have to buy from you in order to avoid any losses the price becomes largely irrelevant.

So what are the big takeaways here?

- **The cost is not important in sales:** People assess prices on what they will lose or gain, rather than the cost.
- **Communicate losses rather than gains:** Establish the value of what you are selling from the buyer's perspective and make sure you communicate what they will lose by not buying.
- **Price is not that important:** Price is only one factor in a buying decision and not the most important one either.

Sources

Bennett, P., Brennan, M. & Kearns, Z. (2003), 'Psychological aspects of price: An empirical test of order and range effects', *Marketing Bulletin*, Vol. 14 pp 1–8

Shoemaker, S. (2005), 'Pricing and the consumer', *Journal of Revenue and Pricing Management,* Vol. 4 No. 3 pp 228–36

See also

Chapter 20 – Closing sales is not necessary

Chapter 22 – Upselling works through customer focus

Chapter 24 – Competitive selling needs low prices

Chapter 30 – Sales promotions are for the powerless

Further reading

Kahneman, Daniel, and Tversky, Amos, *Choices, Values, and Frames* (Cambridge University Press, Cambridge, 2000)

Poundstone, William, *Priceless: The Hidden Psychology of Value* (Oneworld, Oxford, 2010)

30 SALES PROMOTIONS ARE FOR THE POWERLESS

*Promoting to customers who feel in charge
makes them less likely to buy*

Sales promotions are standard fare in sales. Every sales person will have come across a variety of sales promotion techniques from discounts to coupons and vouchers to competitions. Indeed, sales promotions are so commonplace they are seen as 'normal'. Indeed, people come to expect money-off discounts, especially online. On the web, people look for the discounts and expect a 'voucher code' field in the checkout process. There are hundreds of websites that list coupons and vouchers, meaning that many people shopping online never pay the full price for anything as they are constantly seeking out suppliers who offer discounts. Far from discounts being a sales 'promotion' online, these money-off vouchers are now expected and many online shoppers will not use websites that do not offer them.

Even in the 'real world' money-off discounting sales promotions are everywhere. Comedians even crack jokes saying things like 'goodness me, that furniture shop has another sale on'. Many furniture retailers seem constantly to have a sales promotion that is so obviously just another sale that they have become the butt of jokes. The furniture store seems to go from week to week from one sale to the next one.

Furthermore, there are now many 'coupon catalogues' that are printed and distributed with local newspapers or popped through the letter box together with your morning post. Your kitchen noticeboard or fridge is probably covered with discount vouchers and coupons for a wide variety of local retailers. Discounted sales promotions are everywhere you look, online or offline.

Clearly they must work, otherwise why would companies run such promotions? Like many things in sales, though, these sales promotions are done because 'everyone does them'. Sales directors do them because they don't want the competition to gain from them. There is little real thought about many sales promotions. They work, to a degree, everyone does them and a company does not want to lose out to the competition. It is a bit like advertising; most businesses do it, so it must be helpful and besides you don't want your competition to advertise when you don't. In other words, much in the world of sales promotion is based on guesswork and instinct.

Researchers at Pennsylvania State University decided to put sales promotions to the test. They recruited 174 people for a study into booking hotel rooms online. Prior to the actual study people were categorized into two groups – one that sensed it had power and control, and a second group that felt powerless. This was achieved using a standard psychological questionnaire that determines our sense of self-power.

Each group was then shown one of two hotel web pages where they could decide to book. One of the web page options showed a price and an amount of dollars off. The second web page showed the price and the percentage taken off in the sales promotion. The hotel rooms were originally US$225 each, so one promotion was for US$56.25 off, the other promotion was for 25 per cent off.

These various groupings meant there were four elements the researchers could test:

1. Powerful people viewing a discount-based sales promotion
2. Powerful people viewing a percentage-based sales promotion
3. Powerless people viewing a discount-based sales promotion
4. Powerless people viewing a percentage-based sales promotion.

The researchers also tested for the participants feelings of confidence in making the right choice.

What the study showed was that the style of discount offered had no real impact on the people who thought of themselves as powerful. If anything, there was a very slight negative effect of a percentage style sales promotion among the powerful people who marginally perceived this as making the hotel room more expensive.

The research, however, demonstrated a significant effect in the people who had a low sense of self-power. These people sensed a good deal with the discounts offered, but were particularly attracted by the discount reduction – much more so than the percentage drop in price.

The Pennsylvania scientists also looked at the interplay between confidence and the likelihood of purchase. What they discovered was that the more powerful people had a greater sense of confidence but that there was a relationship between confidence in calculating the discount and power. It turned out that confidence was the key that linked power to intention to buy. When people felt more confident that they had made the right price calculation, they were more likely to want to buy.

This study has some important implications for everyone in sales. The research suggests that powerful people are more confident and are therefore more likely to buy, regardless of any sales promotion. In other words, sales promotions are unnecessary for such people; providing them only lowers your income. However, for people with a low sense of power, sales promotions like these discounts clearly do work. The most important finding here was that the promotion should not be in a percentage, but in actual money off – in the case of the study, dollars. When people with a low sense of self-power see sales promotions in actual money off they are more confident about the purchase and are more likely to buy as a result.

One thing that you can do to increase sales is to stop offering percentage-off deals and switch to actual money off. Showing the actual price paid and the amount saved appears to be the approach most likely to lead to a sale from a sales promotion. However, such a technique would only work for the people who have a low sense of power.

For customers who feel they have power, sales promotions will not work. This means you can often ignore sales promotions in negotiations. Sales managers will frequently tell sales teams that they have the capacity to offer discounts if the negotiation is getting sticky. But the customer is already feeling a sense of power in a negotiation, so offering sales promotion discounts as a means of getting the contract is unlikely to help. What will help in these situations, the study suggests, is ensuring the buyer is confident they are making the right choice. Hence spending time on sales promotions for the powerful ought to be replaced with spending time on giving them sufficient information to boost their confidence.

There is, of course, an alternative view on what this research means. You could take it to mean that if you increase the sense of power among your customers they become less amenable to a sales promotion. That, therefore, means that you can stop offering sales promotions. In turn, this means that you will increase your profitability as you will no longer need to offer discounts.

You can increase the sense of power in your customers through techniques such as giving them an online account that they can control. Also, making them a 'key account' with their own manager will bestow them with a sense of greater power. You could also give your customers a 'grading' such as saying 'you are one of our gold star clients'. In other words, by making your customers feel special and that they have some degree of control over their relationship with your company, you raise their sense of power. That means they will not need sales promotions to sway their opinions and you can stop offering discounts that cut into your profits.

It is clear that sales promotions have a limited value for businesses. Just because 'everyone is doing them' does not mean you have to. As the Pennsylvania research shows, they only really work in specific and somewhat limited circumstances. You will be better off in increasing the customer's sense of power and confidence if you really want to secure a sale.

So what are the big takeaways here?

- **Sales promotions are not that valuable:** Sales promotions only work when customers feel they have no power.
- **Customers with good knowledge are not influenced by promotions:** Work out the power relationship between you and your customer and then only use sales promotions if the customer is in a weaker position.
- **Sales promotions do not work in negotiations:** When you are negotiating prices, sales promotions do not work because the customer senses they have some power and when they do that they are not attracted by promotions.

Source

Choi, C. & Mattila, A. S. (2014), 'The effects of promotion framing on consumers' price perceptions', *Journal of Service Management*, Vol. 25 Issue 1 pp 149–60

See also

Chapter 2 – Adaptive selling is vital

Chapter 15 – Buyers behave differently now

Chapter 24 – Competitive selling needs low prices

Chapter 29 – Customers have no idea about prices

Further reading

Cummins, Julian and Mullin, Roddy, *Sales Promotion: How to Create, Implement and Integrate Campaigns that Really Work* (Kogan Page, London, 2010)

www.referenceforbusiness.com/small/Qu-Sm/Sales-Promotion.html

31 SALES COMMISSIONS DO NOT MOTIVATE

*Sales staff are motivated by more factors
other than commission*

Carphone Warehouse in the UK is one mobile phone retailer that does not pay its sales staff commissions. True – they get bonuses dependent upon the overall store performance, but they are not paid particular commissions for flogging products. The reasoning behind this change, which was instigated in 2009, was to make the sales staff independent. No longer would they be trying to sell phones based on the commission they received for specific models. Instead, they would be able to offer customer-centric advice in a fair and unbiased way. Carphone Warehouse has not done too badly using this approach. At the end of the financial year to March 2014, sales had grown 5 per cent on the previous year. The year before had seen an 11 per cent growth too. Not too shabby for a sales force that does not get commission.

Like Carphone Warehouse, several companies work on a no-commission basis. However, many do not. Indeed, several companies now employ sales people on zero hours contracts at an annual salary of zero. The aim is to incentivize them to earn the highest amount they can by selling as much as possible and by getting a slice of the sales in the form of commission. Many sales people work on a commission-only basis.

Sales force compensation is a well-worn path for sales managers. They want to design the best compensation schemes possible, which will attract the right staff and retain them. People move around a lot in the world of sales, meaning that sales directors and managers are constantly having to recruit and train new people, which increases their costs as well as slowing down their department. What sales directors want is a fully engaged sales force that doesn't want to leave. Hence designing the right compensation package is essential for staff retention.

For many firms, though, the focus is on commission. Because sales commission is so commonplace in sales jobs it is seen as part of the normal way of running sales jobs. However, just because everyone else does it, does not mean you have to. Besides, as the example of Carphone Warehouse demonstrates, it is perfectly possible to generate healthy sales without specific commissions being paid.

Researchers at Raajdhani Engineering College, Odisha, India, decided to investigate the role that financial commissions play in sales person performance. They studied 194 front-line sales representatives from the pharmaceutical sector and 56 of their sales managers. Each individual was asked to complete a questionnaire that was designed to find out their motivation to work. Participants also had to answer questions on what they thought about their company, including how well they felt valued by the company and how proud they were of the company. The study also looked at each individual's sales performance.

The results showed that the ease of doing the job was highly linked to sales performance. When jobs are well designed and sales people can do their work in a straightforward way, they tend to perform better. The researchers also discovered that having a sense of belonging or feeling able to work independently did not have any relationship to sales performance. What was fundamental to sales performance in this study was having a sense of 'no pressure'.

This research confirms other studies that show that sales staff who feel under pressure to perform tend to perform less well. The pressure to earn an income on zero hours and zero salary contracts therefore would appear to make it much harder for sales people to perform well. Anything that puts pressure on them, such as targets or no income unless they get a sale, appears to make things worse, not better. This is especially the case if their job is made complicated and they cannot do it easily. Technology issues, for instance, could arise in this situation where sales staff are provided with complex technological systems that they would rather do without.

What this study means for sales managers is that focusing on commissions as a means of incentivizing staff is not the best way of achieving maximum sales performance. True, commissions can motivate, but they are not the best motivator in spite of their widespread use within the sales arena. This study shows that other factors are much more closely linked to sales performance.

You will get higher sales performance from sales people if the job they do is designed well and is straightforward with no complex systems or technology. Also, working in a 'no pressure' environment is important, meaning that the whole notion of targets has to be reconsidered – or at least not putting sales staff under pressure to meet such targets. A further important factor in terms of job design is the need for openness within the company and a clear perspective on career progress. What this all suggests is that when the sales person's job is designed in such a way that they can easily see what to do and can understand how it links to their career they become motivated to sell more.

Many other research studies have produced similar findings – people who enjoy their job tend to perform better in it than those who do not. Financial incentives are lower down the list of priorities for most employees. True, they want to earn as much as possible, but they also want to enjoy their job. Consequently, sales managers need to design incentive packages that include elements relating to career progression and which are not related to any kind of pressure.

One area where many sales managers and directors seek to have influence on sales people is by providing them with a sense of 'belonging'. Indeed, many sales leaders focus on team-building and providing methods by which everyone can feel 'involved'. However, the Indian research showed that this was one of the least important elements in terms of sales performance. Belonging to a team does not appear to be important when it comes to increasing sales. That makes some sense; sales people are independent-minded, generally, because they have to do a lot of work on their own. People who are like this are not very likely to be motivated by team membership. Sales people are much more solitary minded and hence being involved with others is not a strong motivator to performing well.

Even so, they want to be paid well. The issue is whether that pay should come from commission. In several years of studying what employees want, researchers from the University of Tennessee have found that salary is significant – or at least it seems that way. But when the findings are delved into it would appear that salary is merely an indicator of what employees really want. The need to be valued by the company and to provide emotional well-being is what the salary indicates to employees. So even though decades of surveys on what employees want suggests money is the pinnacle of their requirements, it is actually more complex than that.

The Tennessee study confirms a key element of the Indian research in that motivation to do a job is more about the emotional factors of the employee, rather than financial ones. Therefore, sales compensation schemes need to consider how to make people feel good about doing their job, such as easy systems and open career pathways. Do this and your sales performance will increase – though your staff will also expect a good salary.

Focusing on sales commissions does appear to be thinking about the wrong thing when it comes to motivating sales people to perform better. One of the key factors in boosting sales performance appears to be making their job simpler to reduce pressures. These days many sales people complain about over-complicated technology that wastes their time and makes their work more complex. A key focus for sales managers who wish to increase the performance of their sales team is therefore to consider simplifications to technology, or indeed whether it is necessary at all. Anything that a sales leader can do in order to simplify the work of sales people will pay off in terms of increased performance.

At the same time, sales managers and directors could consider how they measure that performance so that any element of pressure is removed or reduced. This will be part of the company's attention to emotional well-being of their staff, which the academic research shows is an important factor in performance.

Sales commissions are potentially valuable, but are not the factor that most sales people look for. They want a well-designed job that they enjoy doing and which is valued by the company at an emotional level.

So what are the big takeaways here?

- **Commissions do not motivate as much as other factors:** Sales commissions are much less likely to incentivize a sales person than other factors.
- **Make non-financial compensation more important:** Reconsider your sales incentive schemes so that financial compensation is less important.
- **Create enjoyable jobs to motivate people:** People are motivated much more by enjoying their job and feeling a sense of achievement than they are by the money the job brings them.

Sources

Sahoo, S. K., Routray, P. & Dash, A. K. (2014), 'Does Motivation Really Count for Sales Force Performance in Pharmaceutical Industry?', *Business and Management Research*, Vol. 3 No. 2.

Wiley, C. (1997), 'What motivates employees according to over 40 years of motivation surveys', *International Journal of Manpower*, Vol. 18 Issue 3 pp 263–80

See also

Chapter 33 – Multiple sales targets are better than one

Chapter 38 – Sales leaders need to learn to manage

Chapter 40 – Sales staff must keep up to date with procedures

Further reading

Cichelli, David J., *Compensating the Sales Force: A Practical Guide to Designing Winning Sales Reward Programs* (McGraw-Hill Professional, 2010)

32 SALES TRAINING DEPENDS ON THE BOSS

Training courses have little impact on sales people unless the boss is supportive

Every sales person will have been on at least one training course. Sales training is a regular occurrence for anyone involved in sales. Some courses are product-related, for instance; others are on more obscure topics, such as the use of neuro-linguistic programming (NLP) in sales situations. Every day, thousands of sales people will be taking one kind of course or another.

Yet, at the same time, every day, sales directors and managers are concerned with how they can get their staff to perform better and sell more. Going on training courses doesn't seem to be linked to reducing the desire among sales leaders for even better performance. Could it be that the sales training is not working? Or, alternatively, are sales leaders simply always driven by the need to increase performance from their teams?

One way of finding out is to look at research conducted by the University of North Texas that was intended to determine which factors influenced sales training. By finding out what factors increased the impact of sales training, this research can help sales managers put the right things into place to ensure that training leads to better results. Far too often sales people come back from training courses only to settle back into the old ways of working. The sales training, therefore, merely costs the company money and takes sales people away from actively selling while on the course, meaning a loss of sales. The poor impact of training courses costs the company a great deal. It is therefore valuable to look at the research from Texas to find out what can be done to ensure that sales training courses are not wasted.

The researchers studied 452 people who were the national sales force of an American cleaning products company. All of them were full-time employees of the company, which only did in-house sales training. This meant that there was no real variation in training, which could have been brought about if a range of external suppliers had been used. This therefore minimized the possible impact of the variation of training quality on the study.

The participants were sent a questionnaire in the post and were asked to complete it and then mail it back to the researchers. The questionnaire looked at a variety of factors in an attempt to find any links between the training and its effectiveness.

First, the questionnaire looked at 'locus of control'. This is a psychological concept that is about the degree to which people feel they are self-determinant; how much of what they do is down to them or how much is due to the influence of others (internal vs external locus of control). The questionnaire also looked at the task self-efficacy of the participants – how capable they thought they were of completing tasks on their own. Another element of the questionnaire was the learning style of the participants – how did they best learn things?

Other factors the questionnaire investigated looked at the climate in which the training was done, the feeling of support from sales leaders and how social the participant was. All of this information was then compared with the sales performance of the people completing the questionnaire.

When the questionnaires were analysed some surprising results emerged. For example, the locus of control was not related to the satisfaction of the sales training. This means that regardless of whether people think they are in control or the external world is in control, the satisfaction of sales training is not connected. You might think that people with an internal locus of control would find the sales training more satisfactory, but this was not the case.

What was related clearly to the satisfaction with sales training was how well people thought they were effective at their job. This self-efficacy rating was closely connected with the sales training satisfaction, suggesting that people who thought they were capable also found the training worked for them.

Another interesting finding was that learning style was unrelated to how well the training course was perceived. This is counter-intuitive; you would expect learning styles and satisfaction with training to be closely connected, yet this was not the case.

The study did show, however, that when people had good peer support during the training course they reported much more positive feelings than when socialization was low. The feeling of being supported by others on the same training course appears to make people rate the training more highly.

The researchers found an additional area that was connected to the satisfaction of training and that was the support received from the line manager and the organization as a whole. In particular, the action-oriented support was much more important than just general feedback, according to the findings of this study. This implies that sales managers and leaders need to be actively involved with the training – finding out what they might need to do as a result of what the sales person has learned, or putting into place anything that is required in a practical sense to allow what has been learned to be effected.

Another important finding from the study, which has practical ramifications for sales leaders, is the need for people to have good peer support (serial socialization as the researchers call it). In essence, this means setting up mentoring schemes, for instance, where more experienced sales people can support and guide those who have just been trained. This will also help in terms of another finding from the research. Training had a good impact when the organizational culture was supportive of training. By having a mentoring scheme in place, this will provide additional help to the impact of training by establishing a positive environment that accepts training as important. In some organizations, for instance, training courses are perceived negatively, merely offering a 'day out of the office'.

The researchers also discovered an important point that was more about the kind of training that was offered by the company to improve selling skills. This was focused on making the customer feel comfortable and general communications skills to build rapport with the client. However, this course was not related to any improvement in sales performance. What appeared to be missing was any improved way of relating specific benefits to customers. The research, therefore, showed that it is not just the role of sales managers to support training initiatives and breed a culture of accepting training, but also to determine the way in which the training is delivered and the content. It is no good sales managers leaving the training to the company's training team – the content of the courses needs to be related to improving sales performance. Perhaps this also means that instead of the typical 'happy sheets', which are the feedback forms collected at the end of the training course, a company needs alternative ways to measure course effectiveness, linking real world performance to specific training courses.

Indeed, what this research really points out is the central role in training that the sales manager plays. Instead of just recommending courses or arranging sales people to go on relevant courses, the sales manager or director needs to be actively involved in planning, delivering the follow-up and arranging appropriate measures of effectiveness. The boss in any sales team, therefore, has a much more pivotal role in ensuring that training has impact than might otherwise be thought.

As a sales manager or director it is important to set the right tone for training to be accepted by sales staff. That means accepting training for yourself as one of these leaders and being seen to have your own training measured. It also suggests that sales leaders need to be actively involved in all aspects of training for their team. Training cannot really be something that is delegated or simply outsourced if it is to have any kind of real beneficial impact. The Texas research was clear. A business that has supportive sales leaders, with peer mentoring and good role models is one that can benefit from training. However, a non-supportive environment where training is just completed for the sake of it is unlikely to provide the right mix to enable the company to actually benefit from the courses. Their costs could be money wasted.

So what are the big takeaways here?

- **Sales training has limited impact without good managers:** Supportive line managers are necessary if sales training is to have any impact.
- **Mentoring and coaching can boost sales training impact:** Create a working environment of mentoring and coaching so that sales training fits into a supportive system.
- **Training on its own does not work for sales people:** Sales training alone does not help sales people perform effectively. It is just training for training sake.

Source

Sager, J. K., Dubinsky, A. J., Wilson, P. H. & Shao, C. (2014), 'Factors Influencing the Impact of Sales Training: Test of a Model', *International Journal of Marketing Studies*, Vol. 6 No. 1

See also

Chapter 31 – Sales commissions do not motivate

Chapter 39 – Customer knowledge depends on sales managers

Chapter 40 – Sales staff must keep up to date with procedures

Further reading

McClay, Renie, *Fortify Your Sales Force: Leading and Training Exceptional Teams* (Pfeiffer, San Francisco, 2010)

Ready, Romilla and Burton, Kate, *Neuro-Linguistic Programming for Dummies* (Wiley, Chichester, 2010)

MULTIPLE SALES TARGETS ARE BETTER THAN ONE

Single sales targets fail to motivate sales people to succeed

Sales targets are normal. Some sales people think they stretch them too far, of course, but companies need them in order to make sure they achieve their objectives. Besides which, sales targets mean that individual sales people can be measured and their performance can form part of their annual review. Additionally, sales people are competitive by nature and so having targets and competing against each other appeals to them.

What kinds of targets work, though? Often, companies will merely add a few percentage points to what was sold one year and ask their sales people to do that amount extra in the next year. Other companies will set unrealistic targets surpassing all possible expectations in the hope that it will stimulate the sales staff to work really hard. Some firms have a highly complex array of targets that are designed to make the sales team pay constant attention to what they are doing, thereby helping them to sell more. Producing the right kind of target or sales objective is a constant issue for sales managers and sales directors.

Research conducted back in 1990, however, provides the answer as to how sales targets work best. The study took place at Kansas State University and looked at the views of 400 people. Each of them was asked to say how they would respond in a variety of sales scenarios. Some of the scenarios had one sales target, others had more than one target. Also included in the study were estimates of risk-taking behaviour by the participants.

The researchers were particularly interested to discover whether there was any relationship between risk-taking behaviour and the presence of more than one sales target. They also wanted to know if the addition of a second sales target was more motivating.

The results showed that when the scenarios included a second sales target – in the form of some kind of bonus for going beyond the initial target – the participants were motivated to perform. The study found that when people know the initial sales target can be easily reached, they behave in a way that makes the second target more likely to be achieved.

The Kansas research also found that when people think they are unlikely to reach the first target, they take more risks in an attempt to reach the second sales target. Conversely, when there is little chance of reaching a second target and even the first target is unlikely to be met, people behave more cautiously.

The researchers found that when a second target was potentially reachable, the target was then something that the participants were prepared to consider. But when the second target was unreachable in their view, it was ignored and they concentrated solely on reaching the first target. The Kansas scientists suggested that this means people are refocusing their attention from the impossible to the probable.

The study confirmed earlier research studies on sales targets, which had demonstrated that sales people tend to want to maximize sales quotas before considering any other targets they may be set. They clearly see the quota as the most relevant and important part of their job. However, once they have met their quota they become focused on any subsequent targets, particularly those that might help achieve bonuses.

There is, though, a complication of having additional sales targets. It tends to increase risk-taking behaviour. Indeed, the risk-taking to try to reach the second bonus target occurs even if the situation means they will not even reach the initial quota target they have been set. Some participants become fixated on the second target and want desperately to reach that even if they are told that meeting the first target is unlikely.

This is an interesting finding because it means if people think the second target is unlikely to be met, they focus on the first target. Yet, if they think the second target cannot be met they become fixated upon it and really want to try to meet it, failing even to reach the first target.

This research has some interesting implications for sales managers and sales directors. It suggests that the setting of targets has a more complicated effect on the behaviour of sales people than might be usually expected. It also implies that having a single sales target fails to help to achieve behaviours that can lead to increased sales; single targets mean that sales people 'play it safe'.

The study also means that the positioning of targets to be reached has to provide a balance between realistic expectations and slightly over-reaching the possibilities so that people strive to achieve the targets without participating in too much risk-taking. Too much risk-taking behaviour can mean that sales people do not even reach the first of their targets, let alone a second one.

Research by the consultancy firm Bain and Co backs up some of what this Kansas study found. Bain discovered that in one firm the successful combination of sales targets was when sales volume was targeted at the same time as sales value. Sales people were then able to work their sales in combination to help them achieve both of these targets. Bain themselves argued that the whole way in which sales and sales targets are managed needs changing.

Many companies continue to use sales models that were only fit for purpose prior to the Internet. More modern technologies have made customers more knowledgeable and less loyal. This means that old ways of setting targets are not always suitable to the new buying environment.

What the Kansas study and the Bain findings suggest is that having multiple or combined factors making up a sales target can work well. However, simply having tiered sales targets does not work because that encourages increased risk-taking, making sales actually less likely, not more.

Setting targets is no longer a simple matter of looking at last year's sales figures and adding 10 per cent. The Kansas research clearly shows that setting targets needs to be more thought through and also needs to take into account the risk-taking profile of each sales person. Indeed, the research implies that the recruitment of sales people needs an assessment of risk-taking so that you can then set appropriate targets for new staff, without putting the company under undue pressure. As the research showed, risk-takers tend to go for the higher sales targets even if they are unreachable. This could impact upon your overall sales, so such people need targets appropriate to their risk-taking behaviour.

You can assess risk-taking in several ways. There are standard psychological questionnaires, for instance, which many HR departments would be using as a matter of routine. Alternatively, there are various risk-taking tests online that you could ask staff to complete to give you a guide. Once you know the risk likelihood of each sales person you can tailor their targets to ensure that they try to sell as much as possible, without taking excessive risks. The more cautious people will need a second target just beyond the reachable first one. However, the people more likely to take risks will need targets that are generally reachable at both levels. In this way you can set them multiple targets they can reach without them having to take risks, which could actually make any of those targets less likely to be met.

Essentially, this all means that sales managers and sales directors need to set individual rather than departmental or team targets. Each of those individual targets needs to take into account the risk-taking behaviour of the sales person. At the same time, targets need to be a combination of factors such as volume and value in order to provide sales people with multiple targets instead of one.

Setting sales targets is not easy for sales managers or sales directors. This research, however, provides a foundation from which to work. First, understand the risk-taking behaviour of your sales staff. Then, set multiple or combined sales targets which work best for the kind of risk-taking behaviour of each individual. This will help you produce more sales at the same time as helping your sales team perform effectively.

So what are the big takeaways here?

- **Sales people need multiple targets:** A single sales target does not motivate sales people.
- **Targets work best when they can be reached:** Establish a range of multiple sales targets that can mostly be reached.
- **Tiered sales targets are less likely to work:** Tiered sales targets, with ever-higher numbers, increase risk-taking behaviour and make it less likely that targets are reached.

Source

McFarland, R. G., Challagalla, G. N. & Zenor, M. J. (2002), 'The Effect of Single and Dual Sales Targets on Sales Call Selection: Quota versus Quota and Bonus Plan', *Marketing Letters*, Vol. 13 Issue 2 pp 107–20

See also

Chapter 15 – Buyers behave differently now

Chapter 31 – Sales commissions do not motivate

Chapter 35 – Sales teams teach each other how to fail

Chapter 38 – Sales leaders need to learn to manage

Further reading

Jordan, Jason and Vazzana, Michelle, *Cracking the Sales Management Code: The Secrets to Measuring and Managing Sales Performance* (McGraw-Hill Professional, 2012)

www.bain.com/publications/articles/is-complexity-killing-your-sales-model.aspx

34 FORECASTING THE FUTURE DEPENDS ON STAFF KNOWLEDGE

Bosses cannot forecast sales effectively without input from junior sales staff

Whichever business or industry you are in, forecasting the likely sales you are going to be able to achieve is fundamental. From a financial perspective this information is needed to plan company-wide budgets, consider recruitment and arrange financial support from banks. Forecasting is also important in manufacturing businesses as the sales forecasts will be used to determine the requirements for raw materials as well as the management of production lines. Sales managers and sales directors might not realize it, but their forecasting has a much more fundamental role for the business than merely setting sales targets.

Working out a sales forecast is not easy, however. It takes experience of an industry or sector as well as excellent research capabilities and good sources of information. You can use a variety of computerized tools to help you produce a sales forecast. Indeed some industries, such as fashion, have well-established computer programs to help forecast sales and plan the entire design, production and logistical difficulties of getting clothes made and into the shops when people want to buy them.

Even so, sales forecasting is notoriously troublesome. Hardly a day goes by without the media reporting that one company or another is reporting that it failed to meet its forecasts. For publicly quoted companies it is essential they inform their shareholders of such problems. The sheer number of reports about unmet forecasts in newspapers and magazines is clear evidence of the difficulties even some of the most successful companies have when it comes to forecasting. Newspaper columnists even bemoan the poor rate of success in forecasting.

So, anything a business can do to produce more accurate forecasts will please the media, shareholders, suppliers, financiers and a whole parade of managers within the business. Sales forecasting is frequently poor, so anything that can be done to improve it will be of real help to businesses.

Research from Bryant University, Smithfield, Rhode Island, USA, has provided an insight into ways in which sales forecasting can be improved. The aim of the study was to find out how sales people could be motivated to contribute to the sales forecasting activity of their company.

The research investigated the opinions of 262 sales people from a variety of different industries and sectors including finance, healthcare, manufacturing, publishing, services and wholesaling. They were asked to complete a questionnaire that was designed to find out how deeply involved they were with sales forecasting as well as how much effort they put into it. The researchers also wanted to find out how seriously the participants took the whole forecasting system and how satisfied they were with it.

The results showed that just over 80 per cent of all sales people do have some role in the forecasting process. However, the bulk of these were people who had worked in sales for between 10 and 15 years – experienced individuals. The analysis of their questionnaires showed that significant factors were important in the motivation of staff to participate well in forecasting. These factors were: how seriously the company itself took forecasting, how much knowledge had been shared about the forecasting process and how much training was provided.

The researchers also discovered that the effort that people put into sales forecasting was largely dependent upon how much they knew about how their input would be used and whether or not they had access to technology which could help them with their input to the system.

Interestingly, the study found that only 14 per cent of people had received any kind of training about sales forecasting. Yet the fact that such training was available and had been used was one of the most significant factors in determining how seriously the individuals perceived sales forecasting. Sales people were also less likely to take their forecasting role seriously when their efforts were not treated seriously by their line managers or their own downstream staff. This suggests that even though some sales people understand the value of sales forecasting it would appear the organization is only paying lip service to their role. The lack of attention paid by sales managers to the forecasting information provided by sales staff is a major reason why sales people did not take forecasting seriously.

When the researchers looked at the satisfaction of sales forecasting, they found that it was the well-trained and well-supported sales people that were the most satisfied. In particular, those who received feedback on their sales forecasting work and were told how their information was being used, were the ones who were most satisfied.

However, the study showed that there was a counterintuitive connection between feedback and effort. When people were given feedback about their forecasting they actually made less effort to do it. The factor that stimulated the most amount of sales forecasting effort was knowing how their work was going to be used by the company.

The results suggest some important areas that need considering by sales leaders. For a start, it would appear that useful information that can help sales forecasts for the company is only going to be forthcoming if the entire business treats forecasting seriously. Otherwise, sales staff would appear to think they are just providing the information for the sake of it. What this means is that for many businesses there is a need to change the corporate culture, making sales forecasting more important generally. In addition, sales staff need to know how their forecasting information is being used and they need to see it being used. They clearly need to be respected for the work they are doing. However, sales managers need to balance the amount of feedback they provide. The research demonstrated that feedback has both a positive effect on how seriously sales people take forecasting but a negative impact on how much effort they put in. Perhaps sales managers need to ask their staff what kind of feedback they require in order to help deliver the right kind, so it does not have a negative impact.

One crucial factor for sales managers is that sales people are much more likely to take part in the whole area of forecasting if they have been on relevant training courses. Sales managers therefore need to consider appropriate training courses for sales staff so that they can improve their ability to forecast and to effectively do the required research and data collection. Few people in the research had been trained, yet these were the ones with significant engagement in sales forecasting.

Another important aspect for sales managers to consider is the need for sales executives to have access to computer programs that can help with forecasting. Sales people said in the research that such programs are of significant help in collating and analysing the information they collect as part of their normal everyday job. The study also found that people found forecasting activities more rewarding when they used relevant and useful computer programs to assist them.

One other feature worth considering by sales leaders is that the research showed no relationship between compensation and the desire to perform forecasting activities. Like other factors in terms of job design, sales people appear willing to undertake forecasting when their work is valued by others and when they are given the tools to enable the work to be done efficiently and effectively. If sales managers were thinking of providing bonus payments as an incentive for completing forecasting activities, then the research showed it is not necessary. What *is* vital is making forecasting processes straightforward with the use of computers and making the sales people doing the work feel valued.

This research provides another instance where it is not money that sales people are interested in. Rather they are interested in doing work that they enjoy and which is treated seriously by everyone around them, especially their line managers. The implication is that by establishing a forecasting culture within the business, more effort will be put into forecasting generally. That can only help increase the accuracy of the company's sales forecasts, which will inevitably have knock-on effects throughout the business.

To achieve all this, though, sales managers need to train more people in sales forecasting and they need to set aside time to share knowledge and involve everyone in a forecasting process that is valued by everyone.

So what are the big takeaways here?

- **Forecasting needs input from sales people:** Sales forecasts are more accurate if sales people are consulted and involved in producing them.
- **Sales people need training in forecasting:** Train sales staff in sales forecasting and information gathering needed for accurate forecasts.
- **Involving sales people in forecasting boosts sales:** Staff involved in the sales forecasting process appear to be more positive and motivated.

Source

McCarthy Byrne, T. M., Moon, M. A. & Mentzer, J. T. (2011), 'Motivating the industrial sales force in the sales forecasting process', *Industrial Marketing Management*, Vol. 40 Issue 1 pp 128-38

See also

Chapter 15 – Buyers behave differently now

Chapter 37 – When to stop selling products

Chapter 40 – Sales staff must keep up to date with procedures

Further reading

Bednarz, Timothy F., *Sales Forecasting* (Majorium Business Press, Stevens Point, 2011)

Thompson, E. (2013), 'Striking a Balance between Sales and Operations in the Forecasting Process', *Journal of Business Forecasting*, Winter 2013-14, pp 29–31

money.howstuffworks.com/sales-forecasting.htm

www.inflexion-point.com/Blog/bid/90329/Why-is-accurate-sales-forecasting-such-a-challenge

35 SALES TEAMS TEACH EACH OTHER HOW TO FAIL

Groups of sales people can teach each other to be 'helpless'

Every year at most companies the sales team gets to go away to a conference or seminar, which is designed to whip them up into another year of top sales. There will be motivational speakers, practical exercises, and lots of 'high-five' whooping and cheering. It is all supposed to engender team spirit and make everyone supportive of one another so that they can all reach next year's targets and get their bonuses. This type of annual sales meeting is so commonplace, it would seem it is accepted as one of the best ways to ensure companies sell as much as possible.

Yet, in spite of the supportive back-slapping and the emotional high it leaves people on, these events might not be the best solution to maximizing sales. Indeed, it is entirely possible that the spirit created by sales teams could be reducing the potential for selling as much as possible. This is because of a phenomenon known as 'learned helplessness'. Essentially, this is when groups of people teach each other to achieve the lowest possible, rather than the highest. Groups of people learn from each other how they can achieve the minimum, rather than the maximum.

This kind of thing happens when people make mistakes that create a feeling of negativity. But those negative feelings get shared, thereby making everyone in the team more negative. Their aspirations become lowered and mutual success is avoided. Social groups often reach a 'level'. Groups tend to reach a 'norm'. This is thought to be a social process that ensures that groups of people stay united, helping to avoid conflict. In a sales team this means that they often reach their lowest possible potential; it can be a race to the bottom all brought about by 'learned helplessness'.

The razzmatazz sales conferences are clearly designed to help avoid this race to the bottom by getting everyone motivated to reach for the top. However, research from the University of Houston suggests that encouraging failure, instead of success, is the right approach to get sales people to sell more.

The researchers initially investigated what happened in several furniture stores in the USA, which employed 537 additional new sales people to add to the significant team. The first study looked at what happened when these new members of staff joined the stores and what impact there was on their selling behaviour.

The researchers interviewed the sales teams every two weeks for a period of six months, giving them a wide insight as well as a fairly long-term snapshot. The sales people were asked what had happened to their sales performance in the previous two weeks and what they expected to be doing in the forthcoming two weeks. In this way the researchers were able to see if the predicted behaviour of each sales person had actually happened.

The study showed that for half of the time during the research, sales targets were not met. Considering that the sales people had already had an average of six years' sales experience before they joined the furniture company, this was not exactly a top performance. To try to see why this might have happened, the researchers also looked at the leadership styles of the sales managers in charge of these sales people.

Not altogether too surprisingly, the study found that the more years of experience a sales person had, the more likely it was that they would predict their future behaviour as being sales oriented and the more likely they would actually behave in that way. In other words, experienced sales people appear to be more likely to think and act like sales people. The researchers also found that as the weeks went by and as sales people failed to achieve their targets, this also made them more likely to want to behave in a sales manner.

However, when the data was considered in combination with the findings about the sales managers, something different began to emerge. It transpired that when a sales manager used a 'transformational' leadership style, it was less likely that sales people would succeed in the long term. Transformational leadership is a motivating kind of leadership. It is where sales managers are supportive, encouraging and motivating. They are meant to inspire their teams to succeed – the kind of leadership that wants those 'rah-rah' razzmatazz sales conferences to encourage and whip up a frenzy.

The research showed that initially the transformational style of leadership did help sales people become more oriented towards selling. However, that impact was short-lived; it did not last through the six months of the study. It appears that sales people who are unable to reach their targets create a cumulative effect on everyone and it is not countered by the positive encouragement of a transformational sales manager. Positive vibes and inspiration only goes so far, it seems – and not far enough to last several months in an environment where half the time people are not meeting their targets.

To further investigate what might be happening, the researchers studied people using Amazon's 'Mechanical Turk' system – an online labour-force of freelance workers. They were recruited to take part in some feedback for a supposed insurance company that was selling insurance to other businesses – a B2B scenario. Each participant was given a scenario in which they had to imagine they had just joined the insurance firm and were being asked to make as much money in the first month as they would do in their normal job. As the participants took part, they were given feedback on their work. This feedback provided the participants with either early or late stage sales target failure. After being told whether their sales performance was good or bad, the participants were then provided with advice from their sales manager. The kind of advice provided differed from participant to participant, with some getting encouragement of the transformational leadership kind and others receiving feedback on avoiding errors or similar neutral advice – neither focusing on the negatives nor providing positive feedback.

This experiment confirmed the results of the furniture store study: when transformational leadership was provided the impact was short-lived. Interestingly, though, this second study discovered that when the sales feedback was focused on the errors, it produced better performance from the sales people. This goes against the whole tide of opinion on workplace feedback, which is geared towards accentuating the positives and encouraging more good behaviour. What this study found was that when sales people have their errors pointed out and ways of overcoming them discussed, their performance improved.

What the study appears to demonstrate is that transformational leadership can help people become more motivated to sell, but that only has a short-lived impact. In many sales environments people fail – they do not meet targets and they get knocked back from potential customers not interested in what they are selling. Given that there is a good degree of negativity in sales, it would appear that the positive impact of transformational leadership is not sufficient to overcome that. This means that in a sales office the negativity can permeate the team with everyone 'teaching' each other to become less successful than they might otherwise be.

So what does all this mean for your sales team? It means that sales targets need to be achievable. Far from stretching people, sales targets need to be possible. Otherwise, the likely failure of achieving those targets means that sales people do not succeed and the team members learn to become as helpless as each other. Unreachable sales targets do not motivate, they just appear to make negativity and lack of success in a team more likely.

Sales directors and sales managers also need to note from this study that transformational leadership styles of support and encouragement have limited impact. Simply having a morale-boosting sales environment does not appear to work, according to this research. It only has a short-lived effect.

Finally, the experiment involving Amazon's Mechanical Turk showed that when negative sales activity is discussed – and people are given options on how to get round it – it becomes more likely that positive sales behaviours emerge. Far from ignoring the negatives and the problems of selling, these are the areas that sales managers ought to focus on if they wish to achieve greater sales in the future.

So what are the big takeaways here?

- **Sales teams can aim low:** Sales teams can suffer from 'learned helplessness', which means they get the lowest they aim for.
- **Goal-setting reduces sales capabilities:** Allow sales people to fail; stop driving new sales people towards goals.
- **Increased sales come from avoiding goal-setting:** Short-term goal-setting does not help new sales staff gain confidence and sell more.

Source

Boichuk, J. P., Bolander, W., Hall, Z. R., Ahearne, M., Zahn, W. J. & Nieves, M. (2014), 'Learned Helplessness Among Newly Hired Salespeople and the Influence of Leadership', *Journal of Marketing*, Vol. 78 Issue 1(January 2014) pp 95–111

See also

Chapter 11 – Persistence pays in sales

Chapter 33 – Multiple sales targets are better than one

Chapter 38 – Sales leaders need to learn to manage

Chapter 40 – Sales staff must keep up to date with procedures

Further reading

Cohen, Elay, *Saleshood: How Winning Sales Managers Inspire Sales Teams to Succeed* (Greenleaf Book Group, Austin, 2014)

www.mindtools.com/pages/article/transformational-leadership.htm

*Ethical behaviour from sales people increases
word-of-mouth recommendations*

It is highly likely that you have landed on some web page
or another that was trying to sell you something that you
thought was somewhat 'dodgy'. There are, of course, plenty of
unscrupulous traders on the Internet, all desperate to part you
from your cash. Their web pages give you some sense of unease.
It often appears they are merely interested in your money and
you are not entirely sure that what they are selling is of the
highest quality. Very few of us are prepared to buy things when
we do not trust the seller. Furthermore, few people are prepared
to pay for things that they believe are unethical, or sold without
ethical principles. Indeed, the 'fair trade' movement has grown
substantially over the past decade since the launch of the World
Fair Trade Organization. This aims to promote an ethical
approach to sales, ensuring that small traders worldwide get their
fair share of profits.

However, it seems that with the rapid growth of ecommerce,
there is an increase in unethical sales behaviour online at the
same time as 'real world' stores are doing their best to show they
support 'fair trade' and behave more responsibly and ethically. It
is the issue of online ethical perception that led researchers at the
WuFeng University in Taiwan to investigate the impact of ethics
and trust on online shoppers.

The research looked at the online shopping behaviour of
548 people who used various online retailers. The scientists
used an online questionnaire to investigate shopping activity
within fashion, travel, groceries, electronics, computers and
entertainment sectors. The average age of these shoppers was

almost 33 years old and around 60 per cent of them were female. Comparing this with data on the demographics of online shoppers it was remarkably similar – most people shopping online are women in their mid-30s. The study sample was therefore representative of the actual online population.

The results of the questionnaire showed that when the participants believed the websites they shopped at were behaving ethically, they also trusted them more. In addition – and backing up earlier research from this group of scientists – there was a direct relationship between perception of ethical sales behaviour and satisfaction with the company. The study also found, significantly, that there was a clear connection between perceived ethical sales behaviour and the chances of people passing on the website to others via word of mouth.

The data from the study also showed that there was a degree of interplay between the various factors related to ethical sales behaviour. When a shopper thought a company was selling ethically, trust went up, as did the likelihood of word-of-mouth recommendation. But there was also a relationship between trust and word of mouth. As people trusted an organization more, so they were increasingly likely to recommend that shop. This suggests that the perception of ethical behaviour, trust and word of mouth are an interrelated set of concepts that work together to help a company improve its sales.

What this study also showed was that ethical behaviour by companies is demonstrated online, when no sales person is visible or present. Previous studies have shown there is a relationship between trust and the ethical behaviour of individual sales people. What this new study demonstrates is that this kind of relationship exists even if no sales person is present. It would appear that trust and the likelihood of word-of-mouth recommendations associated with perceived ethical behaviour can be extended beyond an individual into an entire organization, as represented by their website.

Indeed, the researchers believe that if a website can demonstrate it is behaving ethically, it can foster long-term relationships with customers that would arise following an increase in trust ascribed to the online shop. This is an important suggestion because, as the researchers point out, unethical behaviour is more likely online than in the 'real world'. Human interaction, including the assessment of body language and other non-verbal communication, means that unethical sales behaviour is much less common face to face because it can so easily be spotted. Online, of course, with no tone of voice or facial expressions to analyse, it is much more difficult to spot unethical behaviour. You might therefore reasonably expect unethical sales to be more prevalent online. Combine this with the relative anonymity of the Internet and you can see there is a recipe for unethical sales people to find a market online.

What this research shows, however, is that shoppers can see through all this with ease. They can spot an online store that is unethical, even though they do not have the option to check out the human aspects of identifying potentially unethical patterns of behaviour.

It means that if you run an online store, if you have a website or you sell via an online retailer, you need to demonstrate the highest possible ethical procedures. Otherwise you will suffer from low sales as well as the potentially negative word of mouth that would result from a lack of trust.

People expect greater transparency these days generally. Tightened legislation – for instance in the financial services sector – is forcing sales people to be more transparent too. This study from Taiwan demonstrates that you cannot really avoid being ethical and transparent about what you are doing. If you do not strive for transparency it means reduced trust, less word of mouth and inevitably fewer sales. There is also the reputational impact on your business to consider.

Sales people, though, are often driven and motivated to 'get the sale' almost 'no matter what'. This means they can often cut corners or do things that bend the rules, just to get the sale. Increasingly, that's the kind of sales behaviour that is disliked by customers. Even if it costs them more or they have to wait longer, most customers want sales people to be completely ethical.

Sometimes that is going to mean being open and honest about sales commissions, for instance. Or it may mean being truthful about the source of the raw materials or the manufacture of the item being purchased. Studies of ethics in relation to sales show that what people expect are truthfulness and full disclosure. Online, people also expect their privacy to be respected and retailers to take steps to prevent fraud.

Clear signals of trust are also expected online. This means having a secure website with the little 'padlock' sign demonstrating it has high security measures in place. It also means explaining at each step of the transaction exactly what is happening, how much it is costing and any other relevant information.

People also expect to be able to email the company for further information regarding their transaction or to have a 'live chat' option so that they can get immediate responses. In fact, lack of immediacy and being able to get answers to questions is a reason for diminishing trust levels in a website.

These are all factors that are measures of ethical behaviour in the real world, of course. When buying something in a face-to-face situation we always have the option to ask questions and to be provided with detailed information about each stage of the transaction. The expectation of your online customers is clearly not a lot different to the requirements of the people you deal with in the real world. There is no need to focus on technology in terms of online sales; what is needed is to consider what people expect from you in terms of demonstrating trust and reliability and then make sure you deliver that online, as you would do in the real world.

What was clear from the research, however, was the importance shoppers place on ethical sales. They do not wish to deal with websites – or sales people for that matter – that are 'on the edge'. This means that for some companies it might require a change of culture. Some sales operations are focused so much on sales, at almost any cost, with a sales force that is pushed harder and harder each week. That can lead to unethical behaviours, which will inevitably work against the firm in terms of sales and reputation. Such companies need to consider how they can change their sales culture, making themselves more trustworthy as a result of increasing their transparency and ethical nature.

Indeed, if companies in the 'real world' continue to behave unethically or 'on the edge', they can expect their customers to use the online world to spread negative word of mouth using social media. Never before has it been so important that sales teams adopt a completely ethical approach to selling.

So what are the big takeaways here?

- **Ethical sales behaviour has significant impacts:** Selling ethically increases trust, word-of-mouth recommendations and customer satisfaction.
- **People check out your ethical behaviour online too:** Adopt an ethical sales approach, both offline and online.
- **Ethical behaviour can be the difference customers seek:** Buyers faced with similar products or services seek a point of difference to distinguish between them. An ethical approach is an effective point of difference helping a sale become more likely.

Source

Hsiu-Fen Cheng, Ming-Hsien Yang, Kuo-Yung Chen (2011), 'Elucidating the ethical sales behavior in electronic commerce', *Journal of Computer Information Systems*, Vol. 52 Issue 1 pp 87–95

See also

Chapter 9 – Key accounts need knowledge

Chapter 18 – Get inside the mind of your buyer

Chapter 26 – Mindfulness can cut conflict

Chapter 28 – Perfect pitches come from mood setting

Further reading

Jones, Graham, *Click.ology: What Works In Online Shopping and How Your Business Can Use Consumer Psychology to Succeed* (Nicholas Brealey Publishing, London, 2014)

Tovey, David, *Principled Selling: How to Win More Business Without Selling Your Soul* (Kogan Page, London, 2012)

37 WHEN TO STOP SELLING PRODUCTS

Do not rely on gut instinct to decide when to stop selling products

Not everything you sell is going to be on sale forever. Products and services come and go. Indeed, if they did not we would all still be wearing smelly dead animal skins, using parchment and travelling on horseback. New products mean progress. They also mean profits. Businesses have to constantly come up with new ideas for products and services. Otherwise, they are likely to be facing competitive pressure they do not want. Plus they will be seen as 'old fashioned' and out of step with the times. New products and services are essential for businesses; sticking with the same old products can spell disaster for companies.

However, just because you have a new product does not mean you need to give up the old ones you have been selling. After all, some people still like those old things you are selling; there is always a market for them. Yet, if you continue to sell your old products and services as well as the newly invented ones, you'll have a problem. You will soon have a sales inventory that is too difficult to cope with. Not only will sales people be expected to remember a constantly growing list of products, but they'll also have difficulty in coping with such a wide variety of samples.

A further issue with having too many products on sale is related to manufacturing. A wide variety of products can cause difficulties with supplies of raw materials. It can also lead to stock-related problems such as shortage of space, or the need to hire bigger premises to house the growing array of products. Even if you are in the services sector there are stock and storage problems, because each of your services needs things like manuals, brochures and so on. Space and its decreasing availability is a consideration even within the services sector.

These are just some of the reasons why you have to stop selling some products and services and move on to something new. Quite apart from the need to be seen to be innovative and 'leading edge', there are the practical problems of having too many old products and services hanging around.

Most firms have some kind of 'product life cycle'. A new product arrives, it has a 'life' and is replaced by a new model or version or an alternative after a period of time. Some sectors have short product life cycles, such as the world of books and publishing, whereas other sectors, like pharmaceuticals, tend to have a long product life cycle. Whichever sector you are in, though, somebody somewhere in the firm has to decide when to take a product away from sale.

Sales people often have mixed views about this. Sometimes they are concerned that an 'old faithful' that is a sure seller is removed from the inventory. On other occasions they are worried that they have nothing new to offer their customers, making the company look out of touch. Sales people, of course, like to offer their advice as to when new products are needed or when old products should be phased out. After all, they are at the 'sharp end', hearing what customers are saying. Sales people are often in a great position to have an informed view as to whether or not a product can be removed from sale.

However, there are other considerations a business needs to make, such as the impact on the supply chain processes or the competitive situation. Sales people – in spite of having their 'ear to the ground' in the marketplace – are not always best placed to make a decision about product retirement. Then again, neither are the people in manufacturing, logistics or marketing. They may have very good reasons for stopping a product that would conflict with the recommendations of a sales person.

Someone does have to make a decision, though, and this is what formed the basis of a study conducted at Ajou University, in

South Korea. The engineers there wanted to see if there was a mathematical way of calculating when to stop one product and move on to a new one. They considered the application of 'fuzzy logic' in helping to calculate a decision for sales people.

Fuzzy logic is a mathematical concept that you encounter most days, often without realising it. Fuzzy logic, for instance, is used in the controls or your washing machine, or in your car as it has to decide how best to use fuel. Fuzzy logic helps control trains, it is used in vacuum cleaners and is also helping seismologists predict earthquakes. Ordinary logic only has two answers – yes or no, true or false. So, for instance, your kettle is either on or off. It can't be half-on, or a quarter off. It is one thing or the other. But what if your kettle needs to know when to cut off the electricity requirement according to the water temperature? In that situation the water can be 'almost hot enough', 'just a bit too hot' or 'quite hot'. There is no longer a 'yes or no' answer, but a 'maybe', a 'nearly', a 'perhaps' kind of answer. Yet electronic controls of all kinds need an answer; your kettle needs to know when to cut off its electricity, according to the rising temperature of the water. There is no right or wrong answer here, it all depends. This is the basis of 'fuzzy logic' – providing answers based on something that cannot be yes or no.

To see if fuzzy logic could be applied to product life cycles, the engineers in Seoul decided to test it out on a fictitious scenario involving electronics products. Using mathematical analysis of past product life cycles the scenario was put together to provide as realistic a situation as possible.

In the first phase of the analysis, the only input into the decision-making was from the sales department. This included data on the sales volumes as well as intelligence on the marketplace. The next phase of the analysis included the thoughts of a person who was given the ranking of products in terms of their sales potential. They were also given information on the strategic importance of the products to the company. In a final phase of the study, another individual used an analytical 'dashboard' produced by the engineers to elect products for cessation.

What the researchers were able to show was that using this combination of techniques involving fuzzy logic it was relatively straightforward to produce a much more informed decision as to which products to stop selling.

The Korean engineers produced a complex mathematical model that clearly worked in the confines of an academic study. However, for most office situations it might be too complex or cumbersome to operate. What the research did show, however, was that taking sales data on their own is unlikely to produce a useful or accurate method of making a decision about when to retire a product.

This means that sales directors need to take into account an array of different factors before making any kind of recommendation to withdraw a product from sale. Not only do they need plenty of feedback from sales people, they also need information on sales volume, quantities ordered and so on. Together, all this information can help, but as the Korean study demonstrated, this single-level approach to making decisions about ending a product life cycle is not adequate.

Instead, the decision needs to be taken in conjunction with people on other teams, such as those in manufacturing or logistics. While many companies will already discuss product life cycles across a variety of teams, they do not always do so together with the kind of complex mathematical modelling the Korean researchers did. Discussing ideas with one another is one thing; analysing the situation mathematically is another. While that may not be possible in many firms, it demonstrates that deeper consideration needs to be given to product life cycles than is the case for many companies.

It means collecting as much data as possible and then using this to make informed decisions. Basing decisions on 'gut instinct' could lead to items being taken off sale that could continue to sell and make profits. Or it could lead to items remaining on sale that have a limited market. A true sales leader, therefore, takes a wide view of product life cycles, ensuring they have considerable input from their sales team and data from a variety of departments before they make a recommendation about ending a product's life.

So what are the big takeaways here?

- **Decisions on when to withdraw products need data:** Deciding when to stop selling a product should be done based on more than just 'gut instinct'.
- **Data collection is essential on all aspects of product sales:** Collect all kinds of data on product sales and usage to help make informed decisions about products and whether or not to stop selling them.
- **Out-dated products must be withdrawn as soon as possible:** Continuing to try to sell out-dated or out-moded products and services means you reduce profits as a result of increased costs.

Source

Jeongsu Oh, Jeongho Han & Jeongsam Yang (2014), 'A fuzzy-based decision-making method for evaluating product discontinuity at the product transition point', *Computers in Industry*, Vol. 65 Issue 4 pp 746–60

See also

Chapter 2 – Adaptive selling is vital

Chapter 38 – Sales leaders need to learn to manage

Chapter 40 – Sales staff must keep up to date with procedures

Further reading

Masao Mukaidono, *Fuzzy Logic For Beginners* (World Scientific Publishing, Singapore, 2001)

Saaksvuori, Antti and Immonen, Anselmi, *Product Lifecycle Management* (Springer, New York, 2002)

38 SALES LEADERS NEED TO LEARN TO MANAGE

Managers and directors need to provide clear development guidelines for teams

Unless you work in a company where you are the only sales person, you will have a manager of some kind. In big firms, of course, there may be several sales managers leading particular teams. They might not be called 'sales managers'; they might be 'team leader' or 'product manager' or some other title, but whatever they are called the principles are the same: their job is to get their sales team to sell more.

The problem with this over-arching requirement of all sales managers is that it is rather vague. Everyone knows that the objective is to sell more, but how are sales managers meant to achieve that? In earlier chapters you can discover that the trend for motivational sales management that uses 'transformational leadership' is actually working against businesses – it doesn't help people sell more.

Often, people end up in a sales management role because they are good at selling. Their track record of high performance means they are the 'obvious' candidate to put into a job where their knowledge of selling can be used to help more junior members of staff to succeed. The problem is these people are good sales people, not necessarily good managers or motivators.

This whole issue of what sales managers need to help them manage their teams was investigated by researchers at the University of Toledo, Ohio, USA. They studied 206 sales managers from 10 different companies in America. Most of them were quite new to sales management with only two years in that role; however, the average experience in a sales job was more than a decade. Their average age was 37 and almost three-quarters of them were male, thus reflecting the current typical profile of a sales manager.

The participants in the study were given several different ways in which their role as sales managers could be improved. They were asked to comment on each possibility as well as to rank them in order of usefulness to their particular job.

The number one requirement was clarity on what they were expected to do. The sales managers in the study wanted to know from their managers and directors more precisely what their job entailed. Indeed, 81 per cent of participants said this was the most important help they could receive in order to help them manage their team more effectively. Understanding what they were being measured on would appear to provide the clarity that sales managers need in order to lead their teams to appropriate success.

The next most commonly requested requirement by sales managers was having effective appraisals and reviews of their own performance. Most of the participants in the study said that their company did not put appraisals very high on the agenda, yet for 74 per cent of the sales managers having a regular, high-priority review of their performance was necessary.

The sales managers in this study also said they wanted to be challenged. They didn't want to 'just manage', they wanted to be involved in more aspects of the business and they had ambitions, which meant they needed to be able to show their strengths.

This was linked to the notion that career pathway planning was important for the sales managers in the study. This was the fourth most popular requirement of the participants. Clearly they want to be challenged and show their strengths, but this appears to be linked to the fact that they want to know where they can head next in terms of their career. Rather than this being ad-hoc and just part of general discussions in the office, 68 per cent of the participants in the study said it was necessary to formalize this.

They also wanted more formal feedback and coaching from their own managers and directors. While the participants tended to agree that the appraisal of their role was essential, they also wanted much more regular feedback on what they were doing right or wrong. Part of this could come from mentoring, said 60 per cent of the participants in the study. Others were more specific, saying they wanted to use the 360-degree feedback approach.

Another factor that would clearly be part of the development of the manager's personal abilities was involvement with professional associations. Such organizations provide the learning opportunities that many sales managers (58 per cent in this study) clearly want.

This research is clear. Sales managers from across a variety of companies and sectors want the same thing. They need to know how well they are doing. To achieve that they also need to be set crystal-clear guidelines, rather than vague notions of just managing a team. They also want regular feedback, support in helping them improve their knowledge and skills and a clear career pathway.

Many businesses, of course, already think that they are providing guidance for their sales managers. However, this study is clear that they want more. In particular, they want increased clarity and much more measurement on specifics as well as feedback on how they are doing, together with guidance on how to achieve more. The participants clearly respect their own managers and directors because they want them to act as their mentors and show them how to progress to their level. These sales managers are obviously ambitious and want to be challenged and supported to help them achieve their personal goals, in addition to the corporate ones.

For many companies this means considering several changes to the way they organize and lead their sales managers. It suggests, for instance, that sales managers need much clearer targets above and beyond a notional sales target. They want to know more than this; they require clear objectives on a variety of management issues. Plus they want to be able to be measured against these goals so that they can check their progress in achieving them. This means that sales directors need to be much more specific in what they want their sales managers to do. It has to be considerably more than just getting a team to sell more if these sales managers are to perform well.

Furthermore, sales directors and other senior managers clearly need to set aside more time to manage their managers. The sales managers want more feedback from their own managers. Plus they want regular coaching and mentoring from the senior directors they respect and admire. Sales directors need to realize that feedback and appraisal is not just part of the annual review. Instead, ambitious sales managers are expecting this to be something that is almost a daily feature of their work. They want sales directors to be more engaged with giving them feedback and guidance so they can continue to improve.

Another area for sales directors to consider is the design of the job that they give to sales managers. The sales managers in this study clearly want to be challenged. This suggests that sales directors need to add tasks to jobs that are not always considered to be part of the sales manager's role. For instance, helping to develop new product ideas or involvement in setting up new territories or teams are both tasks outside the scope of most sales manager job descriptions but would be the kind of challenge they would relish. Regularly adding in extra challenging tasks for sales managers is something they clearly like and feel they need to help them develop and manage their own team.

They also need time away from the office to be involved in professional associations. Sales managers want to be involved in such organizations to help them learn and improve. This means that sales directors need to set aside time for sales managers to be able to take part in conferences, workshops and seminars run by professional bodies. It also means in many companies that a change of attitude or culture might need to be planned, because all too often attendance at such events is seen as a 'jolly', a day out of the office, instead of the learning opportunity that sales managers perceive.

Another attitude change that might challenge sales directors themselves is to realize that many sales managers want their job. They want to learn so they can take on more senior roles. Sales managers are ambitious people and so sales directors need to set aside time to help them plan their career and assist them in reaching their personal goals.

The University of Toledo research is clear – sales managers want their bosses to manage them and help them develop. They want clear guidelines, they want regular feedback, they want advice and support and they want to learn and improve. Companies need to organize their own systems to provide sales managers with much more personal support than is often the case. Once that is done and the sales managers feel much more supported, they can then manage their teams more effectively. It appears from this research that if a business wants to sell more, one way of achieving it is to take a much more personal approach for managing the sales managers.

So what are the big takeaways here?

- **Sales leaders need training and support**: Sales leaders need development too if they are to manage their teams effectively.
- **Leadership skills are essential for sales leaders**: Arrange training and development programmes for sales leaders, focusing on their leadership skills and management capabilities.
- **Expectations need clearly setting for sales leaders**: Sales managers need to know exactly what is expected of them if they are to be able to lead a sales team to success.

Source

Longenecker, C. O., Ragland, C. B. & Mallin, M. L. (2014), 'Developing high performance sales managers: key practices for accelerating growth', *Development and Learning in Organizations*, Vol. 28 Issue 2, pp 10–13

See also

Chapter 35 – Sales teams teach each other how to fail

Chapter 39 – Customer knowledge depends on sales managers

Chapter 40 – Sales staff must keep up to date with procedures

Further reading

Lepsinger, Richard and Lucia, Anntoinette D. *The Art and Science of 360 Degree Feedback* (John Wiley, San Francisco, 2009)

Yemm, Graham, *The Sales Book: How to Drive Sales, Manage a Sales Team and Deliver Results* (Pearson Education, Harlow, 2013)

39 CUSTOMER KNOWLEDGE DEPENDS ON SALES MANAGERS

Financial performance of sales teams rises when managers create the right culture

Several studies over the years have repeatedly shown that companies do not know as much as they think they do about their customers. It is no shock to most sales leaders that their sales executives could know more about their customers. Often it is surprising how little sales people do know about their customers. When customers are asked why they buy certain products or services from a company their reasons do not always match up with what the sales people think is behind their motivation. It is as though the sales person doesn't understand the customer much at all.

Knowing your customer thoroughly means you can anticipate their requirements. It means you can act in a consultative way and, as a result, sell more to them. Excellent customer knowledge means more sales. Getting to know your customers as well as you possibly can produces financial rewards.

None of this is new to sales managers or directors. They are regularly saying that sales people need to get to know their customers better. Yet, in spite of this, companies frequently fail to focus on understanding their customers as much as they know they ought to be doing.

Canadian researchers at Brock University, Ontario, decided to investigate what was needed in order to help sales teams gain more customer knowledge. Their theory was that it was something related to the way the sales team was managed. They believed that if the sales manager behaved in a certain way, sales teams would be able to gain more customer knowledge. They also felt that if there was an increase in customer knowledge, there would also be a commensurate rise in financial success. That would mean that the sales success of the team would depend upon the way in which the sales leader managed the process of customer knowledge.

The research was conducted in Turkey, the 16th leading economy in the world and one of those that has undergone substantial growth in the 21st century. The researchers selected a company involved in the manufacture of building materials to study. The company sold its products through 92 different distributors around the country. Many of these used key account management in addition to their normal sales procedures. Of the 92 distributors, 80 took part in the study, which provided survey data from 259 sales managers who had an average team of 3.3 people. These managers were aged around 41 years old and had been running their teams for almost eight years. Almost all of them were graduates.

The survey was written in English but translated into Turkish and the translation triple-checked to make sure it was an exact reflection of the original. Two key elements were being scored in the questionnaire. The first of these was the level of 'empowering leadership' – how much freedom and autonomy was provided to the sales team members by each leader. The second item being scored by the questionnaire was the amount of customer knowledge creation that was taking place by the sales teams – how well were they getting to know their customers.

The sales leaders also had to provide information on financial performance as well as information on how the teams had to work together, or not. In addition, the researchers wanted to know what the customer relationships were like.

With all this information the analysis was able to show that there was indeed a link between financial performance of teams and the style of management. In addition, the customer relationship performance was also linked to the style of management.

The main significant finding was that the degree of 'empowering leadership' was connected with the amount of customer knowledge creation. In short, this means that sales managers who empowered their staff to be independent and make their own decisions enabled them to also create more customer knowledge. This suggests that giving staff a greater degree of freedom in their work somehow allows them to get to know their customers better.

There was also an interesting twist to this finding. When the researchers looked at the degree to which sales staff could operate independently it was found that when their tasks were interdependent the ability to create customer knowledge went up significantly. What this means is that when each sales person could not do tasks without input from other sales people their knowledge about their customers went up. Working together, doing tasks that need input from others, significantly contributed to the growth in customer knowledge.

Looking at the data on financial performance and customer relationship performance, the Canadian researchers found a clear connection between these factors and their earlier analysis. What they discovered was financial performance and customer relationship performance were both connected to the way customer knowledge creation took place. In turn, of course, that is related to the way sales managers manage through empowerment.

In short, what this study shows is that a sales manager who empowers their team, providing them with greater freedom, is the kind of manager that helps the team to generate more knowledge about their customers, leading to increased financial performance. In other words, you make more money in your sales team if you provide them with greater freedom. However, there is another important factor that makes this all work and that is the degree of task interdependence. Empowering staff without jobs that are interdependent could be the wrong approach. What this study in Turkey found was that people who were dependent upon each other for tasks were the ones that created most customer knowledge. That means the financial benefits of empowering staff are only likely to arise if they can truly work together as a team.

In practice this study has several implications for businesses. For a start it means that sales teams with more customer knowledge capability tend to do better financially. It is proof that knowing and understanding customers is what makes for better sales; that much is well accepted by sales leaders. However, it is the area of job design that is worthy of special consideration by sales leaders. The benefits of good customer knowledge only surface when teams truly do work as a team, it appears. That means companies need to consider how they design the tasks and roles of sales people in order to ensure proper, task-related teamwork. Doing so, however, means increased knowledge creation, which leads to better financial performance.

That said, the research also showed that too much interdependence between tasks can reduce the potential for creating customer knowledge and with it the improved financial performance. There is clearly a difficult balancing act that sales leaders need to consider. Greater teamwork helps, but not so much that the entire array of tasks cannot happen unless everyone is involved.

More important, is the need for sales managers to have an empowering style of management. This happens when sales managers trust their sales people and have the confidence they can do the job. They allow them the freedom to work independently and they respect the views and ideas that they produce as a result of such freedom. It is a far cry from authoritarian leadership styles where managers effectively tell the staff what to do and make them 'follow the rules'. It is also unlike the trendy 'transformational leadership' that supposedly motivates people to perform. Several studies of transformational leadership show that this style of leadership tends not to work in sales. However, empowerment of sales people, giving them a considerable degree of freedom, appears to work as it provides them with the opportunity to build increased customer knowledge, which then relates directly to their financial performance.

There is another aspect to this finding, which was not explored by the Canadian researchers, and that is the role of the Internet. Building customer knowledge is easy online, of course. There are corporate websites to help build knowledge as well as social media, blogs and forums. Sales people are not short of information about their customers. However, many firms restrict Internet access during office hours, especially social networks. The idea is that this prevents distraction, taking people away from their real job. Yet, such a restriction is part of authoritarian management – almost dictating to staff what is right or wrong in the office. Empowered leadership would provide sales people with unrestricted Internet access, believing them capable of handling the distractions themselves. It is interesting to consider, therefore, that in providing unrestricted Internet access sales managers are actually providing their teams with a source of information that helps them increase customer knowledge. In authoritarian management, Internet access becomes restricted, thereby reducing the potential for customer knowledge creation. The very tool that can help sales people learn more about their customers, leading to greater financial performance, is only going to be completely available if empowered leadership is in place.

So what are the big takeaways here?

- **Sales managers create the sales culture**: Sales managers can create a culture of customer knowledge that increases the financial performance of a sales team.
- **Sales managers should allow staff more independence**: Empower sales teams by having a style of leadership that allows for more independence.
- **Sales team freedom increases financial measures**: Empowered sales teams gain more knowledge about their customers, which is linked to increases in financial performance.

Source

Menguc, B., Auh, S. & Uslu, A. (2013), 'Customer knowledge creation capability and performance in sales teams', *Journal of the Academy of Marketing Science*, Vol. 41 No. 1 pp 19–39

See also

Chapter 35 – Sales teams teach each other how to fail

Chapter 38 – Sales leaders need to learn to manage

Chapter 40 – Sales staff must keep up to date with procedures

Further reading

Goleman, Daniel, *The New Leaders: Transforming the Art of Leadership* (Time Warner Paperbacks, London, 2002)

Sasso, Coach Joe, *Sales Team Leadership: Pure and Simple* (iUniverse, Bloomington, 2012)

www.inc.com/kevin-daum/8-tips-for-empowering-employees.html

40 SALES STAFF MUST KEEP UP TO DATE WITH PROCEDURES

Constantly being updated on techniques and systems boosts sales performance

Excellent sales people always seem to have the latest news and knowledge. They know what their customers are doing and clearly read their blogs and news items about them. Furthermore, they know the ins and outs of their own company's brand new products or services, which have only just been launched. They also appear to know 'the latest' on the company's competitors. There appears to be nothing on which they are not up to date. They know everything there is to know, it seems.

However, sometimes such knowledgeable individuals appear to be remarkably inept at certain things. Their brains are crammed full of information that is really useful in their sales job, yet they are sometimes unable to fill in an order form correctly, annoying the sales administrators into the bargain.

What is happening with such individuals is that they are much better at storing and remembering 'declarative knowledge' than they are at dealing with 'procedural knowledge'. Declarative knowledge is fact-based; it is information you can easily recall and recount to others; procedural knowledge is what you know but cannot articulate.

For instance, if someone were to tell you a joke that you thought was really funny you would have two kinds of knowledge. You would have declarative knowledge because you could recall the joke and re-tell it to someone else. You also have procedural knowledge because you know that the joke made you laugh, yet you are at a loss to explain what it was that made the joke funny. You know when to laugh, but can't really explain why. Similarly, when driving a car you know when you need to brake hard and to stop (declarative knowledge) but you cannot explain what your muscles are doing in your legs and feet to ensure it happens. They just do whatever it is you need them to do.

Several studies in the world of sales have looked at different kinds of knowledge to see if there is a relationship between them and performance. As you might expect, sales people with extensive declarative knowledge do appear to perform better. However, such people might not always have good procedural knowledge – the ability to know what to do. Researchers at the University of Georgia, USA, decided to investigate this aspect of knowledge to see if there was some kind of link between sales person performance and their procedural knowledge.

To test this, the researchers recruited 150 insurance sales people and asked them to consider a telephone sales enquiry and an office-based face-to-face prospect. Each sales representative was asked to explain what they would do in each of these circumstances, having been given detailed information on each potential client. The researchers interviewed each participant and used this as the basis of their analysis. However, the scientists also wanted to provide some additional data and did this using 'if then' scenarios. The participants were asked what they would do 'if' a particular kind of situation was before them. They would respond with what they would do 'then'.

With all of this data the researchers were then able to consider whether or not there was a link between procedural knowledge and other factors in the sales process. What they discovered was that there was indeed a relationship between procedural knowledge and sales performance. The participants with the greatest procedural knowledge had the better sales performance. Indeed, the 'if-then' analysis showed that the best sales performances came from people who went through more levels of 'if then' steps for the hypothetical scenario. In other words, these people knew more things to do and more possibilities than other participants. This suggests that the better sales people are those with the greatest procedural knowledge.

When the researchers dug down into the data, they were able to find some more details that showed how this was happening. The highest performing sales people were able to adapt their procedural knowledge to the specific situation. They were not the kind of people who had to adopt a set of procedures and then did not know what to do if the customer moved the goalposts. Instead, the most successful sales people were those who were able to adapt because they had extensive procedural knowledge. Furthermore, what the most successful sales people were likely to do was more elaborate than the least successful sales people. Not only were the top sales people able to adapt as a result of their procedural knowledge, they also were able to provide multiple solutions because they had so many options available to them.

What the study really demonstrates is that the most effective sales people are those who know a great deal about how to sell, as well as what to sell. Much sales training is focused on the 'what' – providing sales people with declarative knowledge about features and benefits of the products on sale. There is little training on procedural knowledge, getting people to understand more about processes.

The researchers themselves pointed out that the best sales performers will often think through the various process options prior to making a sales call. This appears to help give them options should the discussion with customers go in a particular direction. Without articulating procedural knowledge in some way in advance it would seem that sales people are less capable of performing well.

The implications from this study affect sales leaders and how they train their staff. Much sales training is about declarative knowledge, but as this research points out it is procedural knowledge that makes a difference between good and bad sales performers. It all suggests that sales training also needs to take into account how people can be trained in procedural knowledge. That would involve keeping sales people up to date with procedures and processes, but it would also mean training on things like creative thinking, which would help with the planning of sales calls so that procedures and processes are somehow front of mind.

The research also implies that keeping procedural knowledge at a high level will help a company increase its sales generally. But how do you keep a high level of such kinds of knowledge? One way might be through constant coaching and mentoring of staff. Rather than having regular training courses once every few months – mostly on declarative knowledge – it might be better to have frequent one-to-one coaching from more senior staff that emphasizes processes. That way, such things can be kept in mind. Together with creative thinking training, sales people would be therefore able to retain a higher amount and a richer level of procedural knowledge. That in turn, say the researchers, would lead to increased sales.

The study should be a trigger for sales directors and sales managers to think about the kind of training they provide for their sales teams. Knowing facts about products, customers and competitors may seem impressive, but it is only declarative knowledge. As this study demonstrates, without having procedural knowledge the knowing of all those facts is somewhat limited. It will help sales, but having extensive procedural knowledge will clearly help more.

What this could mean for your company is self-supported training and coaching whereby sales teams help each other keep up to date with processes, for instance. Knowing what to sell is one thing, knowing how to sell is another. What this study confirms is that the 'how' is as important – if not more valuable – than the 'what'.

There is one other factor that this research pointed out, however, and that is whether or not sales people have any desire to learn. Sales people are competitive and are not always motivated to learn; they just want to get 'out there' and sell. That could mean that if a sales leader provides too much learning and coaching it would not appeal to the kind of person who is attracted to a sales job. Sales leaders therefore need to strike the right balance between providing enough training and support to increase procedural knowledge while at the same time not boring competitive sales people who will be less interested in such learning opportunities.

So what are the big takeaways here?

- **Learning how to apply sales knowledge is vital:** In sales environments it is not new knowledge that matters as much as how to apply that knowledge.
- **Coaching sales staff helps them focus on knowledge processing:** Provide a coaching environment that helps sales people improve the way they process knowledge, not just acquire it.
- **Sales staff need regular updates on systems and processes:** Knowledge of systems and procedures is linked to increased sales performance. Keeping up to date with systems is as important as keeping up to date with knowledge.

Source

Leigh, T. W., DeCarlo, T. E., Allbright, D. & Lollar, J. (2014), 'Salesperson knowledge distinctions and sales performance, *Journal of Personal Selling & Sales Management*, Vol. 34 Issue 2 pp 123–40

See also

Chapter 34 – Forecasting the future depends on staff knowledge

Chapter 35 – Sales teams teach each other how to fail

Chapter 38 – Sales leaders need to learn to manage

Chapter 39 – Customer knowledge depends on sales managers

Further reading

Rosen, Keith, *Coaching Salespeople into Sales Champions: A Tactical Playbook for Managers and Executives* (John Wiley & Sons, Hoboken, 2008)

INDEX